To Reg

Happy 80th Birthday

Lots of Love

Sue
xxx

BORN IN 1945

HOW TIMES HAVE

CHANGED

WILLIAM DEAN & ELIZABETH ABSALOM

D'AZUR PUBLISHING

BORN IN 1945
HOW TIMES HAVE CHANGED

Published by D'Azur Publishing 2024
D'Azur Publishing is a Division of D'Azur Limited

The language, phrases and terminology within this book are as written at the time of the news reports during the year covered and convey and illustrate the sentiments at that time, even though modern society may find some words inappropriate. The news reports are taken from internationally recognised major newspapers and other sources of the year in question. The language does not represent any personal view of the author or publisher.

First published in Great Britain in 2024 by D'Azur Limited
Contact: info@d-azur.com Visit www.d-azur.com
ISBN 9798326249128

ACKNOWLEDGEMENTS
The publisher wishes to acknowledge the following people and sources:

British Newspaper Archive; The Times Archive; Front Cover Malcolm Watson; p7 45Worlds.com; p11 By SAC Neil Chapman (Fighters); By Photo: Air Historical Branch-RAF/MOD (Bomber); Alan Wilson (bi plane); p13 Bruno Guerrero; p15 (crowds) Mrjspence; p21 Donna D; rollercollin; GrandPanjandrum; p23 commandoveterans.org; p27 RAF Museum; p40 Fashion History; p41 Etsy; p41 Quora; p42 Johan Persson;p42 The Enid Blyton Society; p43 Abe Books; p44 PiccoloNamek: p44 Malcolm Watson: P47 londoncouncils.gov.uk; P48 Richard Cannon; P49 www.planet-sputnik.com/english-rose-kitchen-blog; FineArtAmerica; P54 blue17.co.uk; P55 Prisma Watches; P56 The estate of John Hopkins, Bill Brant; P57 Butlins; P60 Malcolm Watson; P64 Alexandre Prévot, DeFacto - Own work, p66 Victor Hugo King; p65 NASA; p64 eBay; p65 Quatro Valvole; p86 MacDonalds; p94 Vintage Dancer; p100 Science Museum; p100 JodyKingzett; p101 NASA; P101 Salvatore Barbera; p105 Eduard Marmet airliners.net; p106 Wadhurst History Society; p120 Atreyu own work; p120 David Merrett; p123 YouTube; p125 Cédric Janodet; p125 Ken Fielding; p131 Juan Solis; p134 Ethical Trekkin; p134 davidoffnorthide; p151 Corporate Finance Institute; p153 Kingkongphoto; p138 This file is licensed under the Creative Commons Attribution 2.5 Generic license; p146 Dave Comeau; p146 John Douglas

Whilst we have made every effort to contact copyright holders, should we have made any omission, please contact us so that we can make the appropriate acknowledgement.

CONTENTS

LIFE IN

Monarch: King George VI Prime Minister: Sir Winston Churchill (to 26th July) Clement Attlee (from 26th July)

Until May 1945, Winston Churchill's inspiring and resolute leadership was guiding the country through yet another year of wartime rationing and austerity where virtually every household item was either in short supply and had to be queued for, or was unobtainable. But there was a huge sense of optimism that the war was won and great celebrations when Germany surrendered on 8th May and Japan on 2nd September.

Queuing for bread (above).
Pre fabricated house (below).

Planning was well under way for the future and thousands of temporary houses were being provided for the bombed out. In July, Winston Churchill, so popular as leader during the war, was ousted by a landslide in the General Election by the Labour Party, with their emphasis on social reform, full employment, affordable housing, social security and health care for all. The community spirit engendered by the war had given a universal feeling that, after victory, the country could not go back to pre-war social conditions.

FAMOUS PEOPLE WHO WERE BORN IN 1945

6th Jan: Rod Stewart, rock singer
25th Feb: Elkie Brooks, singer
30th Mar: Eric Clapton, rock guitarist
20th Apr: Alistair Cooke, historian and author
19th May: Pete Townshend, rock guitarist
17th Jun: Ken Livingstone, politician
10th July: Virginia Wade, tennis player
31st Aug: Van Morrison, singer-songwriter
26th Sep: Bryan Ferry, pop rock singer

FAMOUS PEOPLE WHO DIED IN 1945

31st Jan: Les Adams, rugby league player
20th Mar: Lord Alfred Douglas, poet and former lover of Oscar Wilde
26th Mar: David Lloyd George, former P. Minister
29th Mar: Jack Agazarian, spy
7th Apr: Elizabeth Bibesco, writer and socialite
11th Apr: Cecil Griffiths, athlete.
27th Jul: Alfred Dobbs, politician
31st Oct: Henry Ainley, actor

1945

Born in 1945, you were one of 48.7 million people living in Britain and your life expectancy *then* was about 64.1 years. You were one of the 16 births per 1,000 population and you had a 3.2% chance of dying as an infant, most likely from an infectious disease such as polio, diphtheria, tetanus, whooping cough, measles, mumps or rubella. Although the war had ended, the country was living under unprecedented regulations governing every aspect of life, no-one in your family would be 'untouched' by the war and you would be reliant on rationing and ration books for some years to come.

But, you were at the beginning of a new era and the country was planning for the future and the future was to turn the old 'social order' upside down. In 1945, the standard rate of income tax was more than 40%, a higher rate was charged on incomes over £2,000 and saving was encouraged. The PAYE system ('pay as you earn') had been operating since 1944 and taxes were now deducted from wages by employers each week or month rather than being collected annually or twice yearly. Clothes were rationed but when not 'making do and mend', the government had intervened in the mass manufacture of high street fashions and 'utility' clothing could be bought free of purchase tax.

Newsprint was severely rationed but the popular papers, the **News of the World**, **The People,** the **Daily Express** and **The Daily Mirror**, reached most of the British homes, shaping public perceptions in the aftermath of the war.

Accommodation in cities was often scarce, unscrupulous landlords raised rents, but agricultural workers were provided with Government cottages. Cheap 'utility' furniture was still made; central heating was unheard of, coal fires heated houses – and coal was rationed. Children helped with the harvest; cinemas thrived for entertainment and newsreels and by 1945 although many pubs had closed due to enemy action, 'the local' was still a comforting place to go to - and everybody seemed to smoke!

WAR TIME BASIC RATIONS

On *average*, one adult, per week

Bacon and ham – 4oz
1s 10d worth of meat – about 8oz
2oz butter
2oz cheese
4oz margarine
3 pts of milk
8oz of sugar
2oz tea leaves
1 Egg

JANUARY 1945

IN THE NEWS

WEEK 1 **"New Year, Same Churchill"** A new year marks another emphatic speech by the Prime Minister, who claims that 1945 will *'bring us victory in Europe.'* Churchill spoke with his usual overbearing optimism, amidst calls for strength of spirit.

WEEK 2 **"The German Broadcasting Corporation"** A *'disparaging'* broadcast disguised as a BBC announcement has been confirmed as false by broadcasters, as they spoke of the enemy's 'Arnhem Calling' supposed to erode the moral of the allied troops.

"The Orchestra Played On" There were no casualties when a V Bomb landed behind the stage at a pantomime in a Southbourne theatre. The orchestra continued to play, calming the audience.

WEEK 3 **"Not Negotiable"** The Prime Minister was met with rapturous applause after declaring that the House would be unified against any suggestion of negotiation for peace with the axis powers, and that nothing other than complete surrender would suffice.

"Ulsterman to the Rescue" Amidst reports of severe labour shortages, the Prime Minister of Northern Ireland has pledged to send more labourers across the Irish Sea to aid in the reconstruction of London.

WEEK 3 **"Homes from the USA"** Over 30,000 temporary portable houses are being shipped from America to help combat the severe housing crisis faced by bomb victims in Britain's major cities.

"New and Improved Austins" Thirty new Austin cars are sitting patiently in showroom windows for distributors and dealers to inspect at the company's factory in Birmingham. The new and improved engines are capable of 16 brake horse power.

HERE IN BRITAIN

"Airborne Operations"

In what appears to be a bid to disprove the allegations that the RAF were disbanding their glider regiment, the Air Ministry have announced a new programme in which airmen will take part in airborne operations in gliders. This is no mean feat, as gliders need a largely different skill set to powered aircraft, the project is being approached with enthusiasm by both the army and the air force alike.
The new glider squadrons will take the majority of their airmen from the already large pool of powered aircraft pilots and will be trained extensively in ground combat.

AROUND THE WORLD

"Anti-Blackout Flying Suits"

Hailed as one of the *'best kept secrets of the war,'* the US designed 'anti-blackout' flying suits are being worn by American fighter pilots to prevent them from passing out when coming out of a steep dive.

The extreme G forces felt by airmen during dog-fighting mean that the pressure exerted on them can be as much as seven times their body weight, putting immense strain on the body. The suit fits tightly around the pilot's lower body, where an automatic valve regulates pressure, preventing blood from draining to the legs.

The latest instalment of the Ministry of Information's popular information booklets sees the story of the Merchant Navy put forward in Epic format. The series, highlighting the heroics of various areas within the War Office and Armed Services, is exaggerated in typical propaganda fashion, to stir patriotism and interest in the war effort; a much-needed muster for enthusiasm after six long years of war. This particular story, tells of the trials and tribulations of merchant seamen throughout the war. Riddled with tales of heroics and beautiful illustrations, the Merchant Navy's edition of the public information leaflet maintains the high standard set by its predecessors.

It was one of the many duties of the Ministry of Information (MOI) to issue 'National Propaganda' to the masses, in order to inform and encourage involvement in the war effort. Amongst the many forms of media utilised by the MOI, the most successful became book-like leaflets that both informed and entertained in a largely exaggerated manner. Although the campaign began in disaster, with an internal dispute over copyright issues for documents, telegrams and reports, eventually, the first pamphlet 'Why Britain is at War,' became available for the public to purchase. Having been ridiculed by corporations such as W.H. Smith Ltd, who warned that 'nobody would want to buy it,' subsequent versions including 'The War at Sea' by 1940 had sold as many as 470,000 copies, been translated into three different languages and had been sold across Europe and the Middle East. 'The Battle of Britain' leaflet saw even greater success, selling over 2 million copies worldwide, over 300,000 of those coming in the first week. The implementation of dramatic images and illustrations proved to capture the imagination of people from all over the Empire.

FEBRUARY 1945

IN THE NEWS

WEEK 1   **"Abolition of Domestic Drudgery"** The influence of the *'progressive views of a woman'* have been attributed to the implementation of new bright colours on items in the gas and kitchen planning exhibition.

"Bomb Alley Order" A licence will now be required to carry out any building work costing more than £10, within a *'reasonable working distance to London'* and for those houses that are in urgent need of repair in 'Bomb Alley's' across the country.

WEEK 2   **"Victory Plans"** The military plans preparing for the final defeat of Hitler have been drawn up by the *Big Three* at a military conference in Yalta. Churchill met with President Roosevelt and Marshal Stalin where they discussed the terms for no surrender.

"Ice Cream for Patients" Ice Cream machines are in the process of being installed in war hospitals across the country in the hope that it may be served as a *'general article of diet'* to recovering patients.

WEEK 3   **"Heath Row Airport"** No plans have yet been released for the repurposing of airfields in and around London after the end of the war. Particular interest is on the partially built airfield, Heath Row, whose use as a military base now seems unlikely.

"The Boat Race" Cambridge came through as the underdogs to beat Oxford in the fourth war-time Boat Race. It was run on the Henley Royal Regatta course in front of a crowd of thousands.

WEEK 4   **"Too Good to be True"** remarked the Queen as she viewed a thermostat-controlled oven at the electric kitchen exhibition in London. Her majesty was left bewildered when shown the device, which contains a red light to indicate correct temperature.

HERE IN BRITAIN
"Tinker, Tailor, Teacher, Spy"

An English teacher working in Paris has been charged with the intention to assist the enemy after he was caught supplying literature to the German War Office for use as propaganda. During the trial, Mr Hewitt expressed his guilt and offered to work on countermeasures to misinform German radio channels.

Nevertheless, the verdict marks the first British citizen to be found guilty of fraternising with the enemy throughout the whole war period. It was revealed that Hewitt was still accepting German payment until the end of 1944.

AROUND THE WORLD
"Frogs and Fleas by Air"

Throughout the war, several strange items have been transported by British aircraft, serving even more bizarre purposes. Some of the most unique of these come in the form of animals, tested in the name of medical research. Live frogs have made numerous trips between England and South Africa with *'Water must be changed at Cairo'* inscribed on each box. Fleas from Sierra Leone and guinea pigs for the treatment of smallpox have proved invaluable for medical purposes and the success of the transportation of this various 'livestock' opens up possibilities for after the war.

A SOLDIER'S BEST FRIEND

The old adage that a dog is *man's best friend* is no truer than in the 14th Army in Burma, where soldiers keep pets in their hundreds. There is not a single dog in the Far East that will go hungry if the British Army are stationed there, with mutual agreements being struck between man and animal daily. In return for food and shelter, the men are getting companionship and dispensing pent-up paternal expression in ways that are the closest simulation of home many have felt since the beginning of the war. The wave sweeping across the British forces is no more pronounced than in the Far East, where General Li-Jen, commander of the first Chinese Army, has seven puppies in his ownership.

However, it is not just dogs that the men have taken to keeping, almost every animal, domestic or otherwise, has been tried. An officer in the Burma Intelligence Corps keeps a bear cub, which was unfortunately kicked out from the Hotel Calcutta for eating the end of a bed. An officer from the fifth Indian division successfully tamed a sheep, which now follows and patiently waits for its master during activities and a Sergeant is in possession of a 10-foot python, which is his pride and joy. Almost every unit has some form of poultry farm at its base and at least one somewhat unconventional pet amongst its ranks.

The story of the week, however, comes from a Derbyshire Corporal, who successfully oversaw the birth of several turkeys on the roadside, and he is protecting them to ensure they don't meet the fate of many of their ancestors. When asked, he revealed his plans to take the turkeys back with him to England, where they can live a happy life in the fields of Derbyshire!

MARCH 1945

IN THE NEWS

WEEK 1   **"Scottish Mining Strike"** Many mining pits across Scotland have been left idle or at limited capacity following the strike of over 7,000 workers across the country.

"The Allowances Bill" During the second reading in Parliament for the Family Allowances Bill, members have been promised a 'free vote' on whether the money should be paid to the man or the woman in the household.

WEEK 2   **"Flying Boat"** Information surrounding plans for the largest ever civil aviation, flying boat has been released. The boat will be capable of transporting 50 – 100 passengers.

"Minesweeping Favouritism" East Coast holiday resorts are accusing the government of favouritism by clearing south coast beaches of mines first, saying no more than half their beaches will be open for Easter.

WEEK 3   **"Raising the School Age"** The Minister for Education has spoken of raising the required schooling age to 15, ahead of the original date of April 1947. However, this will be entirely dependent on the ability to recruit more teachers.

"Hat Conscious" Over 5 million cheap hats will be on sale for women in less than a year. Under a price restriction scheme, designed to make the public more 'hat conscious', the hats will be marked in shops with a star.

WEEK 4   **"Scotland Yard or Hollywood?"** In a new venture by Scotland Yard, a short film entitled *'Man on the Beat'* has been making the rounds in partnership with the British Council. The film, depicting the daily life of being a 'bobby' has been a 'howling success' in 23 languages.

HERE IN BRITAIN

"Victory for The Motor Interests"

Following the war time record of 10,000 motoring deaths last year, the Pedestrian's Association is concerned that this figure will only continue to rise. With the publication of the report by the Ministry of War Transport proposing a 30-mph speed limit *'only to be applied with discretion'*, the Association is outraged and claims that the scheme is open to massive exploitation by drivers and traffic enforcers alike. In a statement, they commented that the report marks *'a victory for the motor interests in their campaign to weaken the enforcement of the law.'*

AROUND THE WORLD

"Blockbuster Crimean Conference"

A Moscow film showcasing the success of the Crimean Conference has been received well by the Russian public. Fans particularly enjoyed watching Churchill's thorough inspection of the Russian troops, looking each man in the eye, and seeing President Roosevelt tour the streets by US military Jeep.

Posters advertising the film show the flags of the three Allied powers, representing the unity forged at the Crimean and Yalta conferences. The film is intended to do more than just entertain, instead to educate the public, and strike fear into the retreating German forces.

THE ROYAL AIR FORCE

A WWI Sopwith (top left).
A WWII Spitfire (front right) and
Hurricane (rear right) and a Lancaster
bomber (front left).

Sir Archibald Sinclair has given a rousing speech to the House of Commons describing the achievements of the Royal Air Force throughout the war, including, but far from limited to, the foiling of the German counter-invasion, and the success of the combined Anglo-American offensive on the German oil reserves, which are now in dwindling supply. Although the German use of the V2 bombs has caused the destruction of homes across the South, the work of the RAF in conjunction with the army, has prevented larger scale destruction.

When the war of 1914 started, the aeroplane was a new and untried weapon, strictly limited in its uses and not sure of its role. Rapidly it developed both as a weapon of offence and defence. When the allies mounted their counter-offensive in 1918, the RAF was able to concentrate 1,290 first-line aircraft against its opponents' 340, and, enjoying this air superiority, was able to disrupt the Germans' communications and harass their troops by low flying attacks. When the WWI Armistice came, the RAF was the greatest air force in the world, possessing more than 200 squadrons, 22,647 aircraft of all, 103 airships and a total strength of 291,000 officers and men. After the war the Service shrank to a shadow of its former self but managed to keep many members possessing a pioneering spirit, which in turn, maintained the high standards and increased the prestige of British aviation throughout the world.

At the beginning of this war, we had far fewer planes than Germany and the country has undergone a massive drive to build Spitfires and Hurricane fighters, and Wellington, Whitley and Hampden bombers. All technically superior to the German planes, but it was, nonetheless, a dangerous situation until the Battle of Britain had been won.

APRIL 1945

IN THE NEWS

WEEK 1   **"5,000 Packs of Smokes"** As onlookers watched on desperately, as the equivalent of 5,000 years' worth of one man's cigarettes were reduced to ashes at a NAAFI store in Skelmorlie, Ayrshire. Valued at over £150,000, the cigarettes were destroyed when a fire caused the explosion of matches within the shop.

"Royal Football Fans" The King, Queen and Princess Elizabeth were all present to witness Chelsea win the Football League War Cup South when they beat Millwall in the final 2–0.

WEEK 2   **"The Princess Put to Work"** The King and Queen, accompanied by Princess Margaret, visited the ATS Mechanical Transport training centre, where they watched as Princess Elizabeth, dressed in blue overalls, was hard at work mending an army lorry.

"Death of a President" In unexpected and sudden circumstances, President Roosevelt has died at age 63. The four-time elected President had been voted the most popular ever, and his death will leave a hole in the heart of Americans across the country.

WEEK 3   **"The Wimpey"** The last air raid of the Wellington Bomber, affectionately nicknamed 'The Wimpey' by RAF crews, has been made against railway yards in Northern Italy. The aircraft has been active since the beginning of the war.

"Eggstra-ordinary Record" The Ministry of Food's Director of Egg Supplies has reported that he hopes to increase allocations of eggs this year to 40 per person, compared to the 30 last year. This follows a record delivery of over 22 million eggs from Canada.

WEEK 4   **"Big Ben to Shine Again"** To the cheering of a small crowd of onlookers, and those inside the Houses of Parliament, Big Ben's lantern has been reignited for the first time since the beginning of the war.

HERE IN BRITAIN

"Penicillin in the Air"

Penicillin via inhalation is the new idea emerging from medical professionals. In a report, this alternative method was stated as a possible means for more effective and efficient administration of the drug, which currently is via injection.

It was even proposed that a small ward would possibly be able to be kept under a constant state of sedation with the air being filled with penicillin for sustained periods of time. The technique would not only be more effective in pain relief, but also use less of the drug than injection.

AROUND THE WORLD

"Anxious Wives v Coastguard"

The US Coastguard have reported that the primary hindrance to their surveillance for German U-Boats has been the large number of 'anxious housewives' who ring to report their husbands missing, after not returning at their expected time.

Rather than fighting with enemy vessels, the men more often than not, get carried away with beer and poker aboard pleasure ships, and are merely returning later than originally stated. The Coastguard has warned wives not to contact them unless their husbands are missing for a very long time.

UNLUCKY FOR SOME!

This ship has no deck 13.

Hot Glass Show	15
Oceanview Café	14
Staterooms	12
Staterooms	11

XIII DEATH

LA MORT

The ominous Friday 13th has struck again, in its usual unlucky fashion, as seventeen greyhounds, meant to be racing the following day, fell unanimously ill before their big race. The event, meant to be held at the White City Stadium, with over 5,000 spectators, had to be cancelled. It is safe to assume that the organisers were not best pleased and will be wary of the date before holding another event.

The number 13 and Friday both have an individual long history of bringing bad luck. In the Bible, Judas, who betrayed Jesus, was the 13th guest to sit down to the Last Supper. In Norse mythology, a dinner party of the gods was ruined by the 13th guest called Loki, 'god of deceit and evil', who caused the world to be plunged into darkness. Peoples of the Mediterranean, regarded 13 with suspicion, not being as perfect as 12, which is divisible in many ways.

As for 'Friday', according to tradition, Adam and Eve were expelled from Eden; Cain murdered Abel; St John the Baptist was beheaded the enactment of the order of Herod for the massacre of the innocents, all took place on a Friday. In Chaucer's Canterbury Tales, written in the 14th Century, he says 'and on a Friday fell all this mischance'. Here in Britain, Friday was once known as 'Hangman's Day' because it was usually when people who had been condemned to death would be hanged and the great crash of 1869, when the price of gold plummeted, was on Friday too.

Whilst some would call it irrational, it is common for people to have 'Paraskavidekatriaphobia,' which is the name for a fear of Friday 13th. This condition may have arisen in the White City Stadium event organisers after the events of the weekend.

MAY 1945

IN THE NEWS

WEEK 1   **"Surprise Strike"** Without any warning, over 4,300 tram, trolly and bus men refused to go on duty this morning, in a surprise strike that crippled public transport across the Capital.

"The Final Bell" The very last 'all clear' siren has been sounded, and with it ends 5 years of siren and noise regulation. There will be no more prohibition on hooters, sirens and rattles.

WEEK 2   **"Unconditional Surrender"** The German Foreign Minister broadcast the following announcement: *'German men and women, the high command of the armed forces has today, at the order of Grand Admiral Donitz, declared the unconditional surrender of all fighting German troops.'*

"Diamonds for Mrs Churchill" The wife of the Soviet Commissar for Foreign Affairs has gifted Mrs Churchill a diamond ring adorned with a gold pectoral cross and encrusted with jewels.

WEEK 3   **"Teacher Training College"** Following the war time shortage of teachers from pre-school to secondary level, over 8,000 candidates have already been shortlisted for teacher training colleges across the country,

"Royal Salute" More than 6,000 members of the British Legion, primarily bemedaled veterans of the First World War, spearheaded a two-mile-long procession through London from the Cenotaph to Buckingham Palace.

WEEK 4   **"Kipper Day"** Kippers for tea may well be the rule again as people queued and waited to to buy them from shops across the country for the first time in many months.

HERE IN BRITAIN

"Dresses From Curtains"

'Make do and mend' is having its 'last hurrah' as women across the country are scrambling to put together outfits suitable for victory celebrations. Curtains have been transformed into light summer dresses, and black out blinds, following the end of 'dim out', have been dealt 'good riddance' and made into Hungarian style skirts embroidered round the hems with gaily coloured wool. Laundered 'flower bags' (2s 6d and 3s) are in demand for another fashion. Women are making them into summer pants for their husbands. One bag makes one pair and saves three coupons.

AROUND THE WORLD

"Shakespeare Returns to the Rock"

With a *'terrifically vital'* performance of Twelfth Night, Shakespeare returned to Gibraltar for the first time in over a century. It was March 28th, 1842 that *'the celebrated juvenile actress Miss Davenport, who was presented with the last hat worn by the late Kean after her performance in London'* appeared in Richard the Third on the island, after *'having reposed in Italy from her extraordinary efforts as dramatic star in America.'* The present production by all ranks of all services, has been produced by a *'debating society founded by the more serious-minded troops in 1941'*.

VE DAY CELEBRATIONS

Processions of tens of thousands of Londoners celebrating the German surrender thronged the streets of the capital with people waving flags, climbing on roofs of buses, and holding up traffic. Pleasure craft, tugboats and transport vessels paraded up and down the Thames, creating a picturesque scene as the sun set over the capital. Fireworks, horns, sirens, and anything else capable of making a loud noise or appearance were brought out, in what appeared to be a spontaneous release of six years' of pent-up frustration, fear and restrictions. The Prime Minister, in classic Winston Churchill style, posed for pictures outside Number 10, a 'V' formed with the fingers of one hand, and his hat raised in another, before attempting to leave his home. Police scrambled to clear a path through the celebrators so that his car could move off.

One of each flag from every Allied Nation could be seen in all London districts, and celebrations were especially joyous in areas most severely affected by the war. Damage sustained during bombing raids to so many London suburbs served to only fuel the jubilation of their people, as queues for the bakers, butchers and confectionery stores stretched 'round the block'. As a national holiday was declared for both the 8th and 9th, Sunday transport services were instigated, with extra trains put on to carry the inevitable huge influx of people to the capital, where the 'half-hearted efforts' of police to control the crowds meant that, for the first time in six years, people were able to fully enjoy themselves.

JUNE 1945

IN THE NEWS

WEEK 1   **"Mosquito's Make Record Time"** Britain to India in just over 12 hours is the headline that gripped the aviation industry as four of the RAF's Mosquito aircraft made the 4,600-mile trip from Britain to Karachi.

WEEK 2   **"200,000 Cars"** A minimum of 200,000 private cars are expected to be completed in the next 12 months with 40,000 by the end of this year. Initially, deliveries will be limited as it is not possible to guarantee all necessary labour and materials.

"The Family Allowances Act" Parliament has finally passed the Family Allowances Act granting financial support to families with multiple children. The Ministry of National Insurance will pay five shillings per week for every child other than the eldest.

WEEK 3   **"Demobilisation"** Demobilisation of allied forces are to be implemented today after extensive planning. Ordered and sequential discharge by *'Classes'* are to begin with Class A men which includes those over 50, family men and former prisoners of war.

"Reverse Lend-Lease" The Queen Mary liner, still wearing her war-time grey paint, transported 14,000 American troops back to the US on her first voyage since VE day.

WEEK 4   **"Election Campaigning"** Tumultuous support for the Prime Minister was shown on his first day's tour from Chequers through the heart of the industrial Midlands.

"Lord Haw-Haw" William Joyce, otherwise known as 'Lord Haw Haw', was formally committed for trial under the 1931 Treason Act for broadcasting Nazi propaganda from Germany to Britain during the war. He opened broadcasts saying *'Germany calling, Germany calling'* in an upper-class English accent.

HERE IN BRITAIN

"Shortage of Wire Netting"

The War Department are burying large quantities of wire netting, perfect for the ongoing effort to repair damaged houses and for completing odd jobs. Although a permit is no longer required, the material is still scarce, begging the question of the War Ministry's motives.

The Government reported that salvage officers are told to get rid of the *'unusable material'* in the most efficient way possible. The practice came to light after a man pleaded not guilty to stealing 6 yards of wire, which he had been ordered to dispose of by the War Office.

AROUND THE WORLD

"Ceremony of the Signature"

Delegates from the United Nations Conference queued up to add their signatures to the recently approved World Security Charter. The event in the Veterans Building started at 6am, and wasn't concluded until the mid-afternoon, with Lord Halifax representing the British signature.

Against a backdrop of pale blue stood the flags of the 50 nations, and the documents lay upon a huge round table on which powerful lights played. Press cameras filmed the whole day and the scene, according to onlookers, resembled that of a Hollywood film set.

EISENHOWER - A LONDONER

THE DECLARATION OF A FREEMAN

The Freedom of the City of London confers the right to drive sheep over London Bridge.

Large crowds lined the streets as General Eisenhower visited the Mansion House to receive his honorary 'Freedom of the City of London'. Having been entertained at lunch by Mr Churchill, a tribute was made to the General by the King at Buckingham Palace, when he conferred on him the Order of Merit. Eisenhower is the first American to be made a member of the Order, after it was bestowed on Marshal Foch and General Joffre after the First World War. Membership is limited to only 24. Cheers erupted from the crowd as Eisenhower began his speech from the Mansion House with '*whether or not you know it, I am now a Londoner myself ...*'

Freedom of the City was first recorded in 1237 and is closely tied to the role and status of the Livery Companies. It was, in earliest times, a requirement for all who wished to carry on business within the City. As a result, the privileges attached to the freemen were eagerly sought, while the duties and obligations were faithfully observed. It is still necessary to this day for all liverymen to be freemen of the City and it is the liverymen who elect the Lord Mayor and the Sheriffs of the Corporation of London. It is no longer necessary to be a freeman to work in the City, but from 1835, the freedom 'without the intervention of a Livery Company' could be purchased by nomination of two sponsors for a fee, known as a 'fine', of (now) £100, and is free to those on the electoral roll of the City. There are a number of rights traditionally but apocryphally associated with freemen including the right to drive sheep and cattle over London Bridge and carry a naked sword in public. However, these privileges are now effectively symbolic.

JULY 1945

IN THE NEWS

WEEK 1   **"Austin to NYC"** A 10 horsepower, 4 door saloon Austin car is making its way to a New York car distributor who wants *'all the small British cars they can get".*

                        "Polling Day" Polling stations across the country opened their gates for the first General Election since 1935. Both the Conservatives and Labour are confident of victory.

WEEK 2   **"Milking It"** The milk allowance is set to reduce from three pints a week to two and a half now that milk production has passed its peak for the season. The change comes a fortnight later than last year.

                        "London Ablaze" Thousands of people witnessed a blaze of splendour, rather than the blazing fires the people of London had become so used to, as streetlights were turned on for the first time in almost six years.

WEEK 3   **"Record House Build"** At 10am The Ministry of Aircraft Production delivered the first aluminium house to be erected for occupation to Shirehampton, Bristol. By 2:55pm, the house was built, and ready to be inhabited.

                        "50 Year Manchester Plan" A 50-year plan unveiled by Manchester City Council showing designs for a ring road and a revamped city centre has drawn the attention of the public.

WEEK 4   **"Utility School Shoes"** Children are increasingly absent from school, often for weeks at a time, whilst their shoes are being repaired. The Board of Trade has been asked to help manufacture stronger children's shoes.

                        "Sweeping Labour Victory" In a landslide victory, Clement Attlee was triumphant in the General Election over war time Prime Minister Winston Churchill, who then resigned.

HERE IN BRITAIN

"Tanks in the New Forest"

The ancient Court of Verderers in Lyndhurst held a heated debate over whether the New Forest is to become the 'new Salisbury Plain', allowing the tank training proposed for the region. Residents spoke of the damage already done by tank operations in designated areas, leaving what was once luscious forest *'an absolute desert.'*
The Army says Salisbury Plain is too small and they are looking for alternative training locations, but they are finding much resistance from residents. The agreement was originally that the army would leave following the end of the war.

AROUND THE WORLD

"Bastille Day"

An air of freedom in Paris dominated the celebrations in Paris for their first unoccupied Bastille Day since 1939. The clandestine celebrations of the previous years were made up for with three days of distinct celebration. Military processions during the day gave way to fireworks and bonfires at night, as the Parisian people celebrated their liberation from both last year, and some 150 years previously. Amongst the celebrations, the French military showcased a number of new weapons from America, which brought great cheers from crowds gathered for the event.

THE HALIFAX EXPLOSION

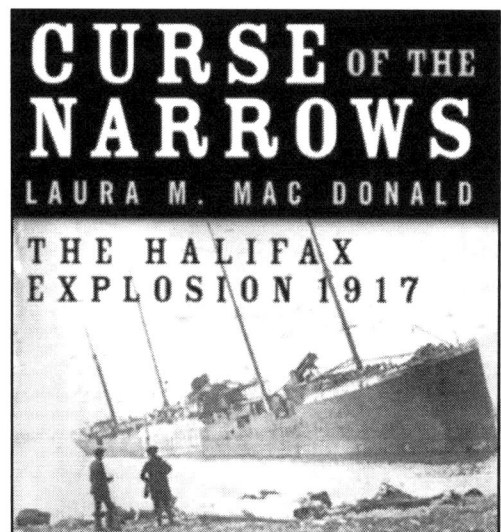

CURSE OF THE **NARROWS**

LAURA M. MAC DONALD

THE HALIFAX EXPLOSION 1917

The Boston Daily Globe

BOSTON, SATURDAY MORNING, DECEMBER 8, 1917—FOURTEEN PAGES

BLIZZARD CUTS OFF HALIFAX 20,000 SURVIVORS DESTITUTE

Trains Carrying Injured to Nearby Places For Treatment and Rushing Aid to Homeless Thousands Stalled in Deep Snow Drifts— List of Dead May Reach 2800 With 3000 or More Hurt

Much of Halifax was flattened by the explosion

A munitions factory explosion some four miles out of the city rocked the Canadian port of Halifax as hundreds of tons of explosives went up in flames. However, this isn't the first time in the 20th Century that Halifax has been gripped by an explosive disaster. In 1917, the port was engulfed with flames when the Norwegian ship *Imo* crashed into a French munitions ship the *Mont Blanc* as it was leaving harbour. Halifax, Nova Scotia was the home of the Royal Canadian Navy during the First World War and became the key transport harbour between North America and Europe for the Royal Navy, shuttling men, coal, food and munitions across the Atlantic. Millions of supplies arrived in Halifax by train, to be shipped to Britain to help with the war effort, and a large number of Royal Navy vessels resided in the port, for refuelling, repairs or rest.

On 6th December, 1917, the two ships collided in the Narrows, the tightest part of the channel, after the *Imo* was forced to the wrong side of the river to avoid oncoming ships. The initial impact set the ships ablaze in a fire that burnt for over 20 minutes, sending billowing black smoke into the air, smoke which drew the people of Halifax and Dartmouth to their windows or the streets ... when the ship eventually did explode, the impact smashed windows across the city, blinding onlookers as shards of glass were sent like arrows into their faces, a gruesome and horrific image that has since been portrayed in *The Curse of the Narrows* by Laura M. MacDonald. Over 1,600 people were instantly killed, with a further 400 dying later from injury. The explosion damaged thousands of buildings and caused a tsunami, even smashing windows in Truro, over 100km away.

AUGUST 1945

IN THE NEWS

WEEK 1   **"For Never Amber"** The novel, *Forever Amber,* has been banned by the Australian Literacy Censorship Board for its *'blatant sexual references',* considering it not a desirable book for the people of Australia. The book has also been banned in 14 American states.

WEEK 2   **"Doomsday"** The US Air Force have confirmed the dropping of the world's first nuclear bomb on the Japanese city of Hiroshima. Japanese news outlets reporting on the devastation cannot yet say the extent of the impact.

         "The Best of British" International demand for British books is once again growing throughout the countries of liberated Europe amidst shortages of paper and transport.

WEEK 3   **"Not So 'Glorious Twelfth'"** August has begun with what has been hailed as the worst opening on record for grouse shooting in Scotland. In the Highlands few moors have been let and in some districts of Argyllshire there are practically no grouse owing to extensive burning of heather to clear the ground for grazing.

         "Bigger Petrol Ration" The Ministry of Fuel and Power has announced that the basic petrol ration is to be increased, with hopes for further allowances in the coming months.

WEEK 4   **"Severn Bridge"** Several million pounds are being put aside for the erection of the 'Severn Bridge' so that work might start soon. Mechanical equipment released from aerodromes is expected to speed up the process.

         "Meals from Down Under" Because rabbits eat grass grown for sheep they are classed as a pest in New Zealand—but they're a favourite dish, too, and now people in Britain will enjoy this delicacy, being shipped along with goat and hare, to help with Britain's meat shortage.

HERE IN BRITAIN

"Nissen Huts"

Nissen huts no longer needed by the army are being sold by the Government for prices starting as low as £3. The huts, measuring 50ft by 16ft, are not suitable for living given their lack of sanitation provisions, but instead are being used and converted even into village dance halls. Farmers, who want them for agricultural storage, village institutions and bowling clubs are among those lining up to purchase the huts, of which hundreds were produced. The corrugated iron shells were mainly used in military barracks for storage and doubled as air raid shelters.

AROUND THE WORLD

"Blinded By Fog"

Air disaster struck in New York City as, blinded by fog and mist, a B-25 bomber crashed into the 79th floor of the Empire State Building. The impact happened at 900ft above sea level, killing 13 people including the three aboard the aircraft, in the crash and the fire which followed.

Luckily, the structural integrity of the building remains intact, but the damage done is estimated to cost £500,000. Because it was a Saturday in the summer, many of the building's 5,000 residents were out, and the number of 'transient' visitors less also.

BEKONSCOT MODEL VILLAGE

The celebrations this week were not limited to V-J Day, the town of Bekonscot, Bucks, reached a landmark 500,000 visitors, all coming to admire the model kingdom of Lilliput, a beautiful micro-picture of quintessential English countryside which has drawn attention ever since its original conception in the late 1920s by Ronald Callingham and his gardener. The model was originally intended as a private miniature park, being formed after Callingham's wife prohibited him from enlarging his model railway inside the couple's house! Eager to continue his hobby, Callingham purchased four acres of land and relocated his railway; from there the project grew and grew, officially opening to the public in 1929, and by 1933, the village was open to visitors every Sunday between April and September.

Whilst the village is fictitious, a number of notable landmarks are dotted across the space, including train stations, libraries, a zoo and even a racecourse, all precisely measured to one inch to one foot scale, perfectly encapsulating 1930s England. An ongoing cricket match on the village green, men out for an afternoon on the golf course and children roughing it up in a boy scouts camp complete the list of fantastic additions to the village. 400 metres of railway represents over 10 miles in real life scale and the money raised from visitors has almost wholly been donated to charitable causes. By 1944, over £10,000 had been raised, creating such a buzz that even royalty came to visit, with the King, Queen and Princess Elizabeth attending on the Princess's eighth birthday.

SEPTEMBER 1945

IN THE NEWS

WEEK 1

"Joy Cables" The stream of free wireless calls, nicknamed 'joy cables', are coming in fast from liberated prisoners of war across Europe and the Far East back to England.

"The Envy of All Countries" The Minister for Health has stated that he plans to equip the country with a new nationalised health system that will be *'the envy of all countries',* but not until after the current housing crisis is resolved.

WEEK 2

"Coffee Ration" Coffee lovers were the only people who could find comfort in the statements from the Ministry of Food, where it was announced that, despite meat rations remaining the same, coffee allocation would increase by a fifth.

"House Rush" A queue of over 500 people could be seen outside the National Housing Trust offices in Birmingham, as they unveiled 400 leasehold houses ranging from £500 to £575.

WEEK 3

"Return of the Restaurant Car" The Minister of Transport has announced the return of the restaurant car on 84 trains across 42 different lines from October.

"Lord Haw-Haw-no-more" The trial of William Joyce, otherwise known as Lord Haw-Haw, has concluded with the defendant being convicted of high treason and sentenced to death by hanging. Joyce was found guilty of transmitting German propaganda.

WEEK 4

"£200 A Second" London raised a staggering £140 million during its Thanksgiving week savings effort, which equates to £200 donated per second.

"Long Socks … Not For You" The long sock trade in Britain is to resume, but with 100% of products being shipped abroad. There is no indication that the Board of Trade will allow the internal sale of long socks in the foreseeable future.

HERE IN BRITAIN

"Stocks of Stockings"

Free pairs of nylon stockings will be available for girls across the country in a new scheme announced by British manufacturers. Over 18,000 pairs are ready to be given to some 2,000 women, who will all receive half a dozen sets each, one for each working day.

The lucky girls are all employees of six British hosiery firms who have been experimenting with nylon yarn, and the women are expected to provide feedback on comfort and utility. The nylon yarn, formerly used for war purposes, is hopefully soon to be widespread.

AROUND THE WORLD

"Golden Cruise"

It has been revealed that two of the largest ever consignments of gold to travel by sea were shipped from South Africa to the United States in the early years of the war. The gold, valued at over £30 million, was transported in two shipments during the height of the Battle of Britain and when U-Boats were at their most prevalent.

After being moved from Capetown to Simonstown under the cover of darkness, the gold was loaded onto a fast cruiser which made the journey to New York in record time.

ADMIRALTY DIVING UNIT

Landing Craft Obstruction Clearance Unit.		
No.	Rank or Rating.	Duty.
1	Lieutenant or Sub-Lieutenant ...	Commanding Officer
1	P.O.	————
2	Leading Seamen	————
13	A.B. or Ordinary Seamen (includes 1 S.D.).	————
1	Signalman or Ordinary Signalman	————
Total	1 officer	
	17 ratings	

Members of the Admiralty Experimental Diving Unit (ADEU) were at the Kingston baths in Surrey, where they demonstrated how a specially trained force successfully cut away underwater obstacles of the 'Atlantic Wall' to facilitate the D-Day landings in 1944. A combination of men from the ADEU, the Landing Craft Obstruction Clearance Unit and midget submarine crews took part in the demonstration exercise, of what has been called one of the most dangerous operations of the entire war.

During the actual mission, some 120 Royal Marines and Navy troops crossed the channel several hours before dawn, before transferring to small dinghies which they were forced to paddle to avoid noise detection. Equipped with 90 minutes' worth of oxygen, the teams dived to assess the level of underwater fortification. 10ft by 10ft steel barricades, 5ft high metal pyramids, pointed steel 'hedgehogs' and underwater mines were just some of the challenges encountered but nevertheless, by nightfall that same day, over 2,400 obstacles had been cleared, leaving a free space of over 1,000 yards. Clearance was done using explosive charges, which were swum from the dinghies with fish like efficiency; it wasn't enough to merely blow up the fortifications, as it required exact calculations to not leave any obstacle which could still be a danger.

For the Kingston demonstration, wooden poles represented obstacles, and the *'frogmen'* as they had been named, were not working from dawn until dusk. Nevertheless, the enormity of the endeavour was made apparent, and the ADEU thanked Dunlop for their superior British underwater suits, especially compared to those of the Germans and Italians. The division has been active since 1933, designed to combat issues of port clearance; although its staff were largely made up from naval personnel and scientists, the unit was only militarised during the Second World War.

OCTOBER 1945

IN THE NEWS

WEEK 1   **"Af-ford-able Motoring"** The Dorchester Hotel in London was the site for the exhibition of two new British-built Ford motorcars. The sales manager announced the updated Anglia and Prefect whilst boasting the cheapest post war production car on sale.

"Return from Afar-east" The first cohort of liberated prisoners of war from the Far East have returned to Britain via Southampton Port; each man received a copy of a 'Royal Welcome Home' endowed with the King's signature.

WEEK 2   **"London Without an Airport"** With three American airline services to begin regular flights from North America to Europe, London is still without a practical commercial airport. The Heath Row terminal will not be completed for at least 18 months.

"Newspapers to Stay Small" The Government ruling to increase the size of newspapers has been indefinitely postponed because of the continued shortage of the necessary supplies. During the war British papers were kept going almost entirely by Canadian newsprint.

WEEK 3   **"One Million Radios"** Britain is set to produce in excess of one million radios in the next twelve months. Although not at the pre-war levels of 1.4 million, over half of these are earmarked to be exported to the Continent.

WEEK 4   **"Across England in 29 Minutes"** The first of two jets that will try for the world's air speed record attempt, flew from Gloucestershire to Kent in a total flying time of just 29 minutes. The two-leg journey saw the Meteor pass over London Bridge at 2,000 feet.

"Nobel Prize" The Nobel Prize for Medicine this year has been awarded jointly to Sir Alexander Fleming, and Sir Howard Florey for their discovery of penicillin.

HERE IN BRITAIN
"Going to the Dogs"

Birmingham City Council has banned dog racing meets on Fridays, or rather, payday. The President of the National Saving's Committee made the announcement this week, deploring the excessive betting on dog racing and its negative effect on the city community.

He spoke of the Committee's experience of seeing men who had lost the entirety of their savings, and it is hoped that the policy will help to prevent such irresponsible expenditure by limiting the funds at participants' disposal. In the last 6 months, over £3.5 million has been placed on dog races.

AROUND THE WORLD
"The Lady with the Shawl"

With Stockholm boasting one of the most famous opera houses in the world, it is little wonder that the people of Sweden are staunch lovers of the events. There is one woman however, who appears to love it more than most.

At the age of 75, Mrs Runnback has clocked up over 7,000 visits to the opera, and is still going strong. She is well known across the city for waving her shawl furiously from her gallery seat at the end of each performance earning her the nickname, *The Lady with the Shawl.*

THE FLYING TADPOLE

The Miles Aerovan (main). George Miles, its designer (inset).

One of the most unusual, yet versatile, aircraft ever produced by British manufacturing, the Miles Aerovan, is to be used to aid export trade in plans released by the Ministry of Transport. This week, an Aerovan landed in Zurich containing over 5,000 fountain pens and is scheduled to give demonstration flights across Switzerland and France later this month. The aircraft, nicknamed the *Flying Tadpole,* has a quirky appearance, but, while its looks may deceive, the Aerovan is extremely versatile, capable of transporting up to ten passengers, goods, and could be used as an air ambulance or even a flying caravan.

The design was conceived by George Miles towards the end of the war, to meet the expected and ongoing increase in demand for air travel and without prior permission from the Air Ministry, he drew up plans and prototypes for the Miles Aerovan. The design was intended by Miles to serve as troop and supply carriers in the Far East during the war, and to then double as civilian airliners after, but the unconventional design was put on hold by the Ministry until now because of its unsanctioned 'birth'. The unusual aeroplane is made predominantly from wood with a high wing and tail design and large rear clam shell doors, helping to gain its name *The Flying Tadpole,* but it wasn't until January this year that a full working prototype made its debut. The original square windows have since been replaced by round porthole ones, and the Berkshire factory has been working round the clock to produce the quota authorised by the Government.

NOVEMBER 1945

IN THE NEWS

WEEK 1   **"World Air Speed Record"** After weather prohibited the attempt last week, Herne Bay was at last the site of the official breaking of the world air speed record. Two Meteor Jets averaged a speed of over 600mph.

"The King at the Cenotaph" London's first official act of commemoration for those who died during *both* wars was held today at the Cenotaph in London and marked by all across Britain on Remembrance Day.

WEEK 2   **"Parachute Clothing"** 26 million yards of nylon, cotton and Celanese parachute fabrics have been surrendered as surplus by the armed forces. Instead, the fabrics will be repurposed and used for much needed clothes production.

"Underground Factory" Details have been revealed by the Royal Institute of British Architects of a factory built completely underground in Britain during the war. Both the cost and time of building was the same as for a surface factory.

WEEK 3   **"Whaling Conference"** An international whaling conference is being held in London to discuss any necessary modifications to the 1937 Whaling Agreement ahead of the 1946-47 season.

"Telephone Demand" The Chairman of the Telecommunication Engineering and Manufacturing Association, speaking at their annual dinner, spoke of the 250,000-person waiting list wanting to get their hands on a telephone for their own home.

WEEK 4   **"Corsets by Christmas"** The war-to-peacetime industry switch has occurred far quicker than first anticipated, with nylon underwear set to be back in shops by the end of the week. Corsets are to be available before Christmas.

HERE IN BRITAIN

"Long Socks Again"

The government provision restricting the length of men's socks is to be lifted, following an announcement by the Ministry of Trade. The restriction was originally imposed in 1942, due to the dire need for yarn to help with the creation of uniforms, warm clothes and equipment for the services, and in the four years since, it is thought that over 6 million lbs of the material has been saved. Though the restrictions have been lifted, manufacturers have warned that it will be many months before long socks will be seen again in shops.

AROUND THE WORLD

"PM's Private Plane"

Former Prime Minister Mr Churchill has been forced to return the plane gifted to him by the late President Roosevelt last year due to its high running costs. Returning the aircraft to the United States *'with regrets'*, Mr Churchill emphasised how public funds are not available given he is no longer Prime Minister, and it was too expensive to justify alone. The plane, equipped with a conference table, kitchen, and cocktail cabinet, needed over £25,000 of repairs and now sits idle in Washington whilst the State Department ponder what to do with it.

FIDO

FOG DISPERSAL

WILL CLEAR RADIATION FOG
FROM RUNWAY UP TO 200FT

CAN YOU LAND
ON THIS?

ASK YOUR FLYING CONTROL OFFICER WHERE THESE ARE AND HOW THEY WORK

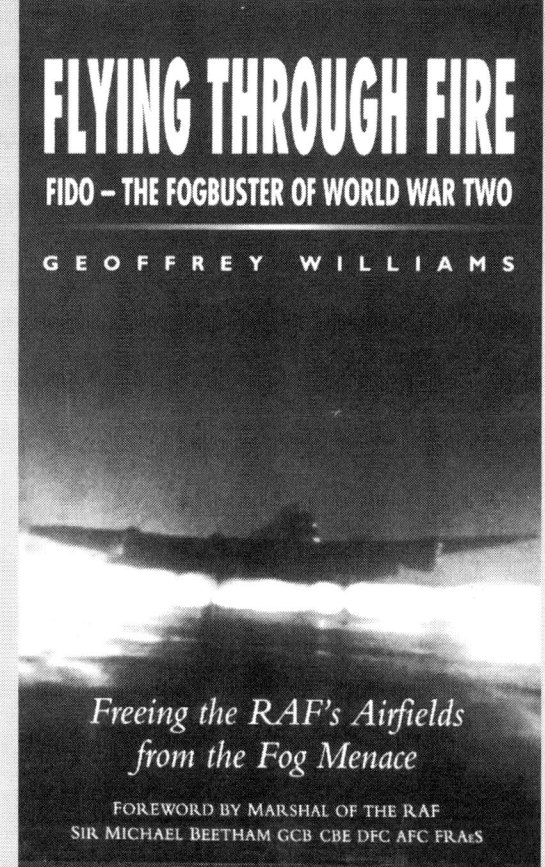

FLYING THROUGH FIRE

FIDO – THE FOGBUSTER OF WORLD WAR TWO

GEOFFREY WILLIAMS

Freeing the RAF's Airfields
from the Fog Menace

FOREWORD BY MARSHAL OF THE RAF
SIR MICHAEL BEETHAM GCB CBE DFC AFC FRAeS

The Minister in charge of Petroleum Warfare who, under former Prime Minister Mr Churchill, was responsible for a number of fog dispersal developments during the war, announced this week the decision of the Ministry of Civil Aviation to stop work on the FIDO fog dispenser, on the grounds of economic viability. Already half completed at Heathrow airport, the Fog Investigation and Dispersal Operation, would have to run for long periods of time, at a high cost, to be at all effective - a cost which the government feels better placed in other areas of public spending.

The device was originally designed to help alleviate fog for RAF Bomber Command aircraft returning from air raids, and the investigation as to its possible commercial uses has been continued by the government. Heat was determined the key to fog clearance, therefore FIDO equipped airfields had runways lined with fuel tanks, pipes and a series of burners that could be turned on and off on demand. When lit, the burners used over one hundred thousand gallons of fuel every hour, roaring and shooting flames so high into the air that they could be seen for over 60 miles. The system was capable of dispersing even the thickest fog within minutes.

Fog, besides the Luftwaffe, was one of the RAF's most formidable enemies during the war, often causing delays, disruption and in some cases, death and destruction, making the job assigned to the Petroleum Warfare Department of the utmost importance. General advice to bomber aircraft crews caught out by thick fog was to fly back to sea but bail out whilst still over land, meaning the aircraft crashed into the ocean. Naturally this was neither a cost efficient nor safe alternative to landing, and with sorties often involving several hundred aircraft, it was not a sustainable procedure.

DECEMBER 1945

IN THE NEWS

WEEK 1　**"The Home of Razor Slashing"** The BBC has been forced to apologise for referring to Gorbals as the *'dockland of Glasgow, home of the razor slashing gangs'*. The *'irresponsible and unwarranted slur'* drew protest from many key Scottish political figures.

"Aircraft Can-Carrier" The first jet propelled aircraft has successfully landed on the flight deck of HMS Ocean just off the Isle of Wight.

WEEK 2　**"Waterloo Bridge"** The new Waterloo Bridge was officially opened after 25 years of controversy was resolved. The bridge has actually been open for pedestrians for over three years and had traffic since November last year.

"Black Cabs" A new design for London taxis has been released, with planned modifications in several areas. The taxicabs of the future will have a lower roof, wider seating allocation and an improved, illuminated, *For Hire* sign.

WEEK 3　**"War Decorations"** Since the beginning of the war, the King has personally presented more than 44,000 decorations to deserving people. However, with a further 55,000 needing to be bestowed, postal delivery accompanied by a signed letter will soon usurp 'in person' deliveries.

"Minor Inconvenience" Several mines have been washed up on the shores of Southern England due to the rough seas and persistent winds.

WEEK 4　**"Christmas at Peace"** The British public were treated to their first peacetime Christmas for six years, and spirits across the Country were high. Nevertheless, they were still forced to *'make a little go a long way'*.

HERE IN BRITAIN

"Secrets of Pepperbox Hill"

Motorists living in and around Wiltshire are familiar with the steep hill climb up Pepperbox Hill, but few know of the secrets that lay hidden within. It was just a couple of years before the war that the Admiralty realised the vulnerability of leaving naval munitions on the ground, where they were susceptible to air attacks. Instead, several sites were earmarked for underground storage spaces, including Pepperbox Hill in West Dean. Thousands of tons of explosives were hidden within miles of tunnelled rock, transported by a narrow train track.

AROUND THE WORLD

"Australian Lights out at 9pm"

Coal strikes across New South Wales have forced authorities to impose restrictions on energy usage for the foreseeable future. Lights out in all dwellings must be no later than 9pm; the wireless will be restricted to just one hour per day; cooking may only take place between 5:30 and 7pm; church services will be required to run under candlelight, and newspaper printing has been suspended. These restrictions were vital to ensure a sufficient electricity and gas supply, which would have run out by the end of this week if not imposed.

THE REGENCY SOCIETY

The Royal Pavilion Brighton

A society has been formed in Brighton and Hove to stem indiscriminate destruction of Regency buildings. Amidst proposed plans for the development of many southern towns and cities across Britain, there are a select few which have highlighted the importance of preserving Britain's rich Regency history. Brighton has become the first place targeted by the Society, who say it is of vital importance to retain the *narrow little streets* of the old town and *harness the past to the future.* The aim of the society is to avoid the sites becoming museum pieces of the future, instead, remaining a quintessential part of Britain that, in 20 years' time, travellers from across the world might visit.

A land mark of Brighton since the 18th Century, the Marine Pavilion was first commissioned by George IV in 1786, when the then young King expressed a desire for a residence in the town. It was actually the King's cook who first purchased the seaside house, along with a substantial area of seafront land. Given Brighton's growing prestige as an aristocratic resort, and the King's fondness for the town after visiting to cure his gout some five years prior, the Pavilion became a serene respite for the Royal Family for more almost a century.

After being converted to a residence more fit for royalty by the architect Henry Holland, the neo-classical Pavilion became home to royal entertainment for three generations of monarchy. King George IV, William IV and finally Queen Victoria all resided in the Pavilion, though it was the Queen who sold the building to the Corporation of Brighton in 1846, instead preferring Osbourne House on the Isle of Wight. Nevertheless, the Pavilion remained useful, with the proceeds from its sale going towards furnishing both Buckingham Palace and Windsor Castle.

THE MAJOR NEWS STORIES

1940:

Jan: Britain calls up 2 million 19 to 27-year-olds for military service.

Jan: Food rationing is introduced in Britain

May: Winston Churchill becomes PM.

Jul: Battle of Britain begins.

1941:

May: Nine months of intensive Blitz bombing ends.

May: First British jet aircraft, the Gloster, is flown.

Jun: Clothes rationing introduced in Britain.

1942:

Feb: The Fall of Singapore to the Japanese.

Feb: Soap rationing introduced in Britain.

Oct: British sailors board a German submarine as it sinks in the Mediterranean and retrieve its Enigma machine and codebooks

Nov: General Montgomery's Eighth Army wins the Second Battle of El Alamein.

1943:

Jan: Utility furniture first becomes available.

May: The 'Dambuster Raid' breaches German dams in the Ruhr Valley.

Dec: First 'Bevin Boys' selected from conscripts to work in the coal mines.

1944:

Feb: PAYE (pay as you earn) system of tax collection introduced.

Jun: D-Day for the Normandy landings. 155,000 Allied troops land on the beaches of France

Dec: The Home Guard is stood down.

1940: Between 26 May and 4 June, the evacuation from Dunkirk of the British Expeditionary Force takes place. 300,000 troops are evacuated, many by little private boats, from France to England.

1941: In February, the luxury liner RMS Queen Elizabeth, now fitted with anti-aircraft guns and with her hull repainted begins her first voyage as a troopship out of Singapore.

1945:

May: Victory in Europe is declared. Celebrations take place throughout Britain. Prime Minister Winston Churchill makes a victory speech.

Jun: The demobilisation of the wartime forces begins.

1946:

May: London Heathrow Airport is opened fully for civilian use.

Jun: The BBC resumes television broadcasting, suspended during the war. Licences are introduced.

Aug: Family allowance cash benefits to mothers are introduced and daily free milk to school children.

1947:

Jan: The Government nationalises the Coal Industry.

Apr: The school leaving age is raised from 14 to 15.

Sep: The University of Cambridge votes to allow women to become full students.

1948:

Jan: The Government nationalises the Railway industry.

Jul: The National Health Service begins, giving the right to universal, free, healthcare.

Jul & Aug: The Olympic Games are held in London.

1949:

Jan: Peacetime conscription in Britain begins. Men aged 18-26 must serve full-time in the armed forces for 18 months.

Jul: The de Havilland Comet, the world's first passenger jet, makes its maiden flight.

1947: The winter was one of the harshest experienced in the British Isles and February was exceptionally cold with heavy snowfalls. It was the coldest February of the century with an average of −1.9 °C (28.6 °F).

1947: In November, Princess Elizabeth marries Philip Mountbatten at Westminster Abbey. The ceremony was broadcast live on BBC television, without sound. The commentary was provided from the studio.

January

28th The German army attempts to make their final advance but are defeated at the Battle of Bulge. From here onwards the Nazis are in full retreat.

February

13th The bombing of the German city of Dresden begins. Thousands of civilian lives will be lost over the next three days in air raids by over 1,300 Allied bombers.

March

7th British and American troops cross the Rhine for the first time.

29th The last bomb of the war is dropped on Britain; a German V1 rocket.

April 25th Russian and American troops meet at Torgau in Germany.

30th With Russian forces less than 500 metres from his Führerbunker, Adolf Hitler commits suicide.

May

2nd Berlin surrenders to the Russian army.

4th The German VII Army surrenders.

8th Victory in Europe is celebrated by crowds taking to the streets all across Allied Europe, America and the Empire. The day has since been celebrated as VE Day all over the world.

11th German forces in Czechoslovakia surrender.

An arranged photo commemorating the meeting of the Soviet and American armies, 2nd Lt. William Robertson (U.S. Army) and Lt. Alexander Silvashko (Red Army) stand facing one another with hands clasped.

April

13th Russian forces enter and capture Vienna.

18th 370,000 German prisoners are taken after the surrender of the Ruhr. All resistance in the area ceases.

SUMMARY

On May 8, 1945, World War II in Europe came to an end. As the news of Germany's surrender reached the rest of the world, joyous crowds gathered to celebrate in the streets, clutching newspapers that declared Victory in Europe.

ENDED IN EUROPE

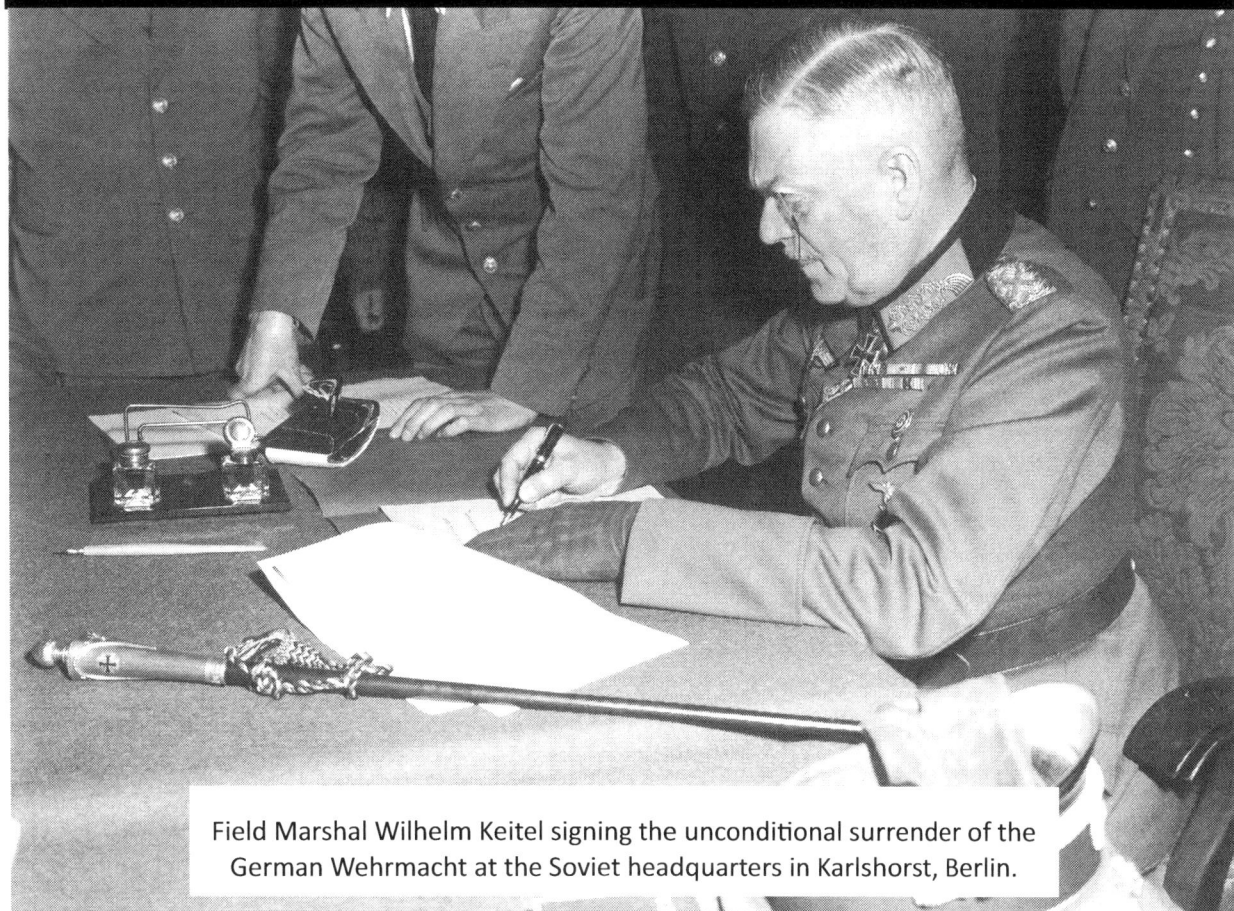

Field Marshal Wilhelm Keitel signing the unconditional surrender of the German Wehrmacht at the Soviet headquarters in Karlshorst, Berlin.

UNCONDITIONAL SURRENDER

Six years of war on a scale hitherto undreamt of was brought to a conclusion with the unconditional surrender of German forces on the 8th May 1945. Now known as *Victory in Europe Day,* the news of the Nazi defeat is still celebrated just as vigorously as it was at the time. Although the outpouring of joy in 1945 represented years of apprehension, fear and suffering, the majority of the British people had been expecting such an announcement since the end of 1944. Plans of 'post-war' Britain had already been put in place, and yet the day still brought mixed emotions for many; aside from the obvious celebrations, people mourned their loved ones as the day came to honour all those who had died in the fighting. It was also important to remember the large contingent of Allied troops still fighting the Japanese in the Pacific. In a speech on national radio, Prime Minister Winston Churchill said, '*We may allow ourselves a brief period of rejoicing; but let us not forget for a moment the toil and efforts that lie ahead*'; a sober foreshadowing of the hardship that was still to come.

Adolf Hitler committed suicide on the 30th April, over a week before the final German surrender. In his place, Grand Admiral Karl Donitz did his best to negotiate terms for the end of the war, desperately attempting to make sure that as few Germans fell into the hands of the Russians as possible. As a result, Nazi occupied Denmark, Holland and Northwest Germany surrendered to Field Marshall Montgomery on the 4th May, followed by the unconditional surrender of all German forces to Allied Commander General Eisenhower on the 7th May; a further document was signed on the 8th in Berlin, thus successfully escaping thousands of Germans from inevitable Russian occupation.

January

19th The Burma Road is reopened.

February

19th US forces land on Iwo Jima, a Japanese island in Operation Detachment. The amphibious invasion comes after months of naval and ariel bombardment. Nearly 7,000 US Marines and over 30,000 Japanese soldiers died in this battle alone.

March

21st British forces regain control of Mandalay in Burma.

May

26th 700,000 incendiary bombs fall on Tokyo as US air raids drop over two thousand tons of explosives on the city in a bid to force a surrender. Over the space of two days, the majority of the city was left in ruins with the destruction of over 16 square miles. Somewhere between 80,000 and 100,000 civilians were killed. The Tokyo raid is the first of further campaigns on another 64 Japanese cities.

June

1st US troops land for the first time on Okinawa. The battle was one of the bloodiest of the whole war, with 14,000 US troops, and 70,000 Japanese soldiers killed. Over one third of the island's entire civilian population, some 150,000 people, were killed in the cross-fire. The US policy of 'island hopping' proved to be too costly for the American government and people, and influenced the decision to use nuclear weapons.

20th Australian troops land in Sarawak.

21st Okinawa is captured by US forces.

July

5th The Philippines is successfully liberated.

14th The Japanese cities of Honshu and Hokkaido are bombarded by the US Navy.

August

3rd Blockade of the Japanese home islands.

6th The world's first atomic bomb was dropped by the US on the Japanese city of Hiroshima. Between 60,000 and 80,000 people are killed instantly, with thousands of other injured. Approximately 67% of all structures in the city were obliterated. The US give Japan an ultimatum, suing for unconditional surrender.

8th Russia declares war on Japan.

9th The second US atomic bomb is dropped on the Japanese city of Nagasaki. Approximately 40,000 people are killed instantly. The second bomb had a 40% larger explosion yield than the first.

12th Soviet troops enter Korea.

14th Japan agrees to Allied surrender terms.

15th Victory in Japan Day.

SUMMARY

Japanese forces were in steady retreat across Burma, Malaysia and the Pacific Islands. They vowed never to surrender and the Allies knew that an invasion of Japan would be difficult and bloody. The use of atomic bombs in Hiroshima and Nagasaki and the Russian declaration of war against Japan forced an immediate surrender.

ENDED IN ASIA

The signing of the Japanese Instrument of Surrender aboard the USS Missouri.

UNCONDITIONAL SURRENDER

It was in July, at the Potsdam Conference, the site where the conditions for the end of the European War were agreed, that there was the first offering for peace in the Pacific arena. Prime Minister Winston Churchill, President Truman and the President of the Republic of China Chiang Kai-shek issued the Potsdam Declaration, outlining terms for the Japanese surrender; these terms were promptly rejected, and it wasn't until the second atomic bomb was dropped by the US on the city of Nagasaki, that the Japanese finally surrendered. In a radio address to the Japanese public, Emperor Hirohito agreed to the Potsdam terms of complete surrender, disarmament, and the occupation of Japanese territory by Allied forces.

Celebrations across Britain and the United States hailed the true end to the Second World War, with President Truman describing the *Victory in Japan Day* as *"the day we have been waiting for since Pearl Harbour."* A two-day holiday was announced in Britain and across the Empire, amidst a period of distinct change, with new British Prime Minister Clement Attlee delivering the news that *"the last of our enemies is laid low"* over British national radio. This was later backed up by the familiar voice of King George VI, who addressed the nation from Buckingham Palace with a celebratory yet sombre tone. *"Our hearts are full to overflowing, as are your own. Yet there is not one of us who has experienced this terrible war who does not realise that we shall feel it's inevitable consequences long after we have all forgotten our rejoicings today."*

Official Japanese Allied occupation began on the 2nd of September, when 13,000 US troops entered Tokyo Bay aboard a convoy of over 40 ships. The Instrument of Surrender was signed by the Japanese foreign secretary on behalf of the Emperor.

Fountain Pen Fuse

MOLDED-IN ANTENNA CAP

OSCILLATOR COIL

PLASTIC NOSE

OSCILLATOR-DETECTOR AMPLIFIER THYRATRON BUNDLE

ANNULAR FIRING CONDENSER

COMPRESSION WATERPROOFING

BATTERY PLATES

RESERVE BATTERY

ELECTROLYTE AMPULE

AMPULE SUPPORT and BREAKER

MERCURY SAFTEY SWITCH

ELECTRIC DETONATOR

COMPRESSION WATERPROOFING

MECHANICAL SAFETY GATE

AUXILIARY DETONATOR HOUSING

No Objection to Publication for Reasons of Naval Security

Review Sect. (Pictorial)
Office of Public Information
NAVY DEPARTMENT

Deemed to be one of the most potent weapons produced during the war, this projectile pen was revolutionary due to its delayed action fuse, known as the *L-Delay*. The fuse, similar in both size and shape to a regular fountain pen, contains a small piece of metal and a striker, separated by a spring, with the time of the fuse depending on how long it takes for the metal to snap once stretched by the spring. It was vital that the metal was of the same consistency throughout, and that the size of the grains that made the tip of the metal did not vary.

The metal, which is a lead alloy, is 7/10th of an inch long and 3/16th of an inch in diameter; in the middle is a neck and it is this neck that breaks and which had to be ground precisely to 1/10,000th of an inch and, after hundreds of trials, the device became exceptionally accurate. The fuse could be scheduled to go off at times ranging from one hour to one month, as long as regular temperature was maintained and as a result, the explosive was used on every front from 1941 onwards.

The Foxer, the Hedgehog and the Sono

Details of Allied countermeasures against the fleet of German U-Boats have been revealed by Naval strategists, with intricate plans and designs culminating in the successful suppression of the German stealth submarines. Devices that enabled aircraft to listen to submarine movements underwater, confuse the targeting systems of U-Boat torpedoes, and mortars that fired multiple depth charges ahead of escort ships are just some of these measures that became so effective.

Not a single Allied ship that towed a *Foxer*, a device omitting sound astern of a vessel, was sunk by U-Boat torpedoes; the *Sono buoy*, a device dropped underwater containing a radio set allowing Allied forces to listen to submarine movements underwater disabled U-Boat's stealth capabilities; The *Hedgehog Mortar*, capable of throwing 24 projectiles over 200 yards ahead of a ship proved to confuse the U-Boat targeting systems.

OF WAR

Decoy Towns

Large decoy fires resembling a town in flames, decoy lighting and dummy airfields were amongst some of Britain's chief defences against German air raids during the war. The schemes, kept a close secret for the duration of the war in Europe, proved to be immensely successful, especially throughout the Battle of Britain and the Blitz in 1940 and 1941. It was estimated that decoy fires lured away 5% of all bombs and mines dropped at night, saving the lives of potentially as many as 2,500 people, and a further 3,000 injuries, not to mention the protection of property and infrastructure.

These decoy towns had the code name *Starfish* and were made up of three different types of flammable material that simulated that of urban destruction. In Cardiff over 150 bombs were drawn away in one night alone by just one *Starfish* facility; in fact, across 730 recorded attacks on decoys, casualties were only inflicted in four. Alongside this, decoy airfields played their part in confusing enemy targeting, to such an extent that by the end of the war, 443 attacks had been made on decoy airstrips, against 434 on real ones.

Firefighters in the London Blitz

D-Day Deception

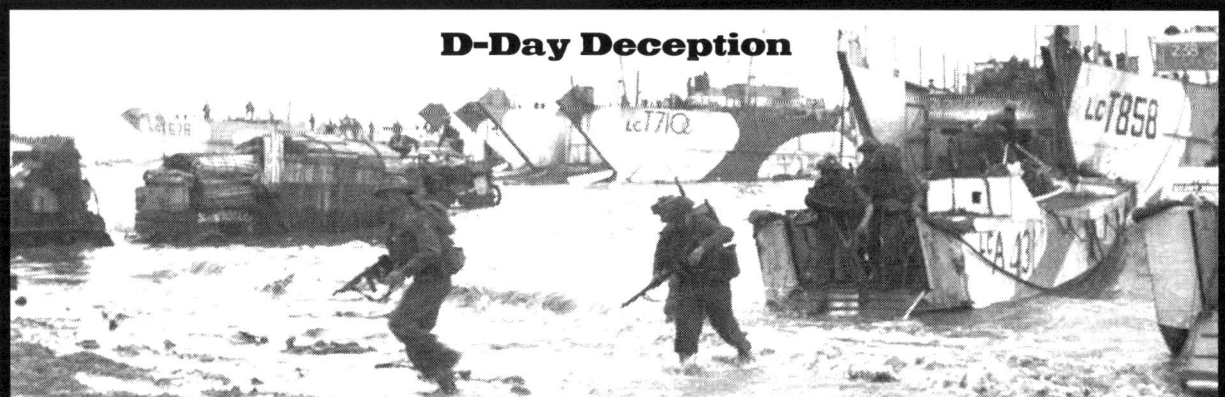

In the weeks leading up to the D-Day offensive, Allied Commander General Eisenhower was placed in command of Operation Overlord, and with that, the strategic deception operation designed to put the Germans off the scent of the true D-Day operation. Eisenhower used several tactics to purposefully mislead the Nazi commanders into thinking the offensive was going to be staged at the Pas de Calais, rather than the Normandy beaches. Not only did Eisenhower 'leak' fake information through double agents, including a wild suggestion of Norway being a key landing spot, but also organised practical deceptions. A 'ghost army' was sent to Calais with a fake Mulberry Harbour - the artificial ports constructed by the allies - in such a way that it diverted attention away from the Normandy beaches, and fraudulent radio transmissions were made.

Entertainment At Home

The radio had been the most important medium for the people to get information during the war but the BBC had also provided much needed enjoyment. In July 1945, the BBC Light programme was launched, concentrating on mainstream light music and entertainment and taking over from the BBC General Forces Programme. **Family Favourites** at Sunday lunchtimes was extremely popular, linking those at home with loved ones who were still away and popular comedy programmes such as **ITMA – It's That Man Again**, **Much Binding in the Marsh** and **The Will Hay Programme**, drew in millions of listeners.

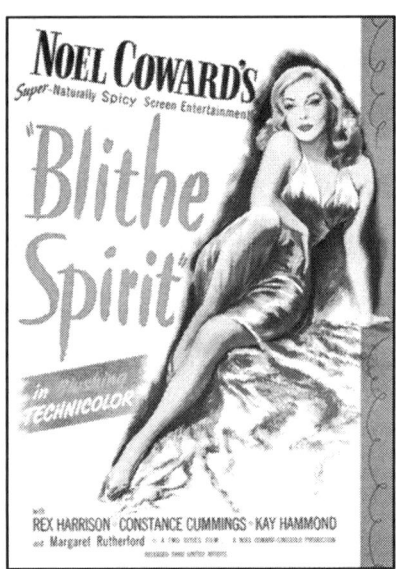

Entertainment Outside Home

The cinema was the mass entertainment of wartime and continued to be so. Again, it had been important for disseminating information but was particularly popular for Hollywood escapism but there were many British films too, romantic dramas and musicals. **The Wicked Lady** with Margaret Lockwood and James Mason had one of the largest audiences of the day, Rex Harrison and Constance Cummings brought Noël Coward's stage play **Blithe Spirit** to life on film.

What We Were Eating

Food was still rationed and seasonal, home grown, food was the order of the day - if you could grow some of your own, so much the better. Newspapers printed recipes and gave advice on how to turn dried eggs imported from America into omelettes, cakes and Yorkshire puddings but dishes were simple and with so little meat available, the nation embraced Spam.

What We Were Dancing To

When the Americans came to Britain, they brought with them exciting new dances such as the Jitterbug and swing bands played in dance halls and even works canteens, giving people the chance to forget austerity and enjoy themselves. In January 1945, a Jitterbug Contest was held with, "Captain Thomas of the US army willing to present One Pound to the winning couple in addition to the Prize."

SHE CAN'T MAKE A HOME TILL SHE GETS ONE . . . SO IT'S—

LABOUR

FOR HOMES

A VOTE FOR LABOUR MEANS A FULL NATIONAL EFFORT FOR HOUSING

LABOUR X

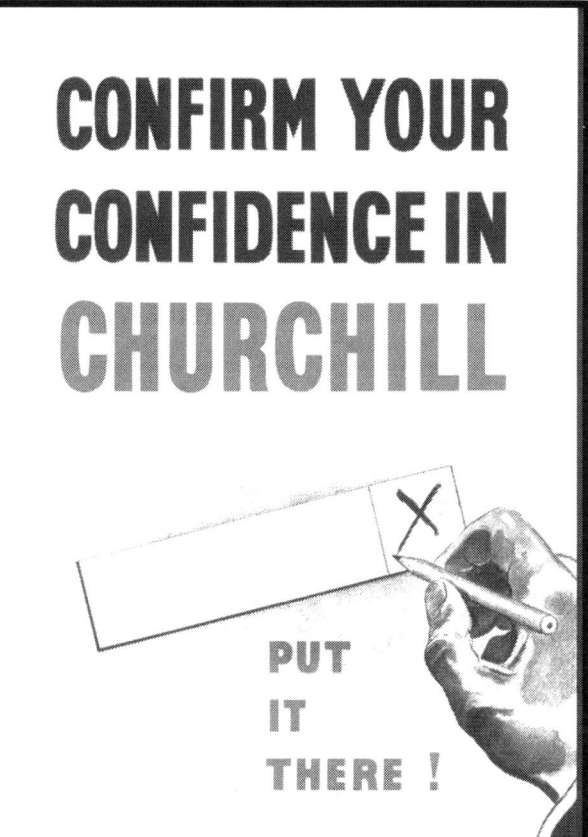

CONFIRM YOUR CONFIDENCE IN CHURCHILL

X

PUT
IT
THERE !

1945 THE END OF WAR - THE END OF A GOVERNMENT

After the jubilation of the two victories and the end of the hostilities, the future still seemed uncertain for the British public. The mines and barbed wire were removed from the beaches, there was no more blackout and the Home Guard, the face of British defiance against Nazi aggression, was stood down. But many things also stayed the same, the war weary nation still faced rationing and Mr Middleton, a radio and TV gardener, continued to urge the nation to '*Dig for dear life*' and to '*force rhubarb, plant potatoes and sow peas*'.

For all the euphoria, Britain was virtually bankrupt, massively in debt to the United States and austerity increased after VE Day, with bacon and lard rations being reduced a few weeks' later, and bread rations introduced in 1946. However, life was going to change and Labour was elected to power in the General Election with a landslide victory, gaining 239 seats, 48% of the popular vote and achieving a majority of 145 seats, thus allowing Attlee to be appointed prime minister. This was the first time that the Labour Party had won an outright majority in Parliament, and allowed Attlee to begin implementing the party's post-war reforms for the country including putting the Beveridge Report of 1942 into action, plans for a new national insurance scheme – the National Health Service – and the 1944 Butler Education Act, which guaranteed the introduction of secondary education for all children.

This decade could be divided into two, up until 1945 and the post-war years. Home life during the war years was very austere and drab and for many, empty, if their children had been evacuated to a safer part of the country. Jobs that before only men would do, women were now doing. Homes were protected with sandbags against explosives; windows were covered with blackout blinds and there were Anderson shelters in gardens. During the whole decade, people listened to the radio, but many people also had gramophones to play 78rpm records.

The war songs remained popular with Vera Lynn a favourite, together with the big bands, swing, jazz and country music from America. Towards the end of the decade, the crooners like Bing Crosby and Frank Sinatra were taking precedence.

Clothes rationing ended in 1954 but materials were still scarce, and fashion was not feasible for millions of women trying to forge a new life after the deprivations of the war.

For those who did, Dior's 'New Look' made the 'hourglass' the shape to aspire to. Skirt suits were popular, with squared shoulders, a narrow waist and tailored skirt that ended just below the knee, and hats, gloves and bright red lipstick, completed an outfit.

In The 1940s

Even when the war ended in 1945, much of the rationing continued. Linoleum was still the king of floor coverings, with a rug in 'the front room'; thousands of families relied on a tin bath in the kitchen for their weekly bath and the toilet was located outside in the garden. 'Colour' was in short supply. BBC television programmes were resumed in 1946 but TV ownership was extremely low and the wireless reigned supreme.

After the war, families did not 'eat out', meals were cooked and served at home, usually to the whole family around one table. Without supermarkets, the woman of the house, shopped at individual butchers, bakers and grocers and the food available was limited and seasonal.

The 'Make do and Mend' mentality endured and during the 1940s you would be hard pressed to find a woman who didn't know how to knit. Lace and airy stitch patterns were a great way to make a little yarn go a long way and it wasn't just wool that was in limited supply, dyes were scarce which meant that colours were limited too.

POPULAR CULTURE

1940:

The BBC Forces Programme begins broadcasting and becomes the most popular channel among civilians at home as well. **Music While You Work** begins in June.

King George VI announces the creation of the George Cross decoration during a radio broadcast. Ealing Studio release the war comedy **Sailors Three.** The song, **All Over the Place** becomes one of the most popular of the war.

A revival of John Gay's **The Beggar's Opera** directed by John Gielgud opens at the Haymarket.

1941:

Noël Coward's comedy **Blithe Spirit** is premiered at Manchester and opens in London in July and becomes an instant success.

The first Ronald Searle cartoon to feature **St Trinian's School** is published in the magazine Lilliput.

London's Queen's Hall, the venue for the **Promenade Concerts** is bombed and the Proms re-locate to the Royal Albert Hall.

1942:

Vera Lynn records **The White Cliffs of Dover** with Mantovani at Decca Records and from America, Bing Crosby's White Christmas is a 'hit' together with Glenn Miller's **Moonlight Cocktail** and **Chattanooga Choo Choo.**

Serge Koussevitzky, Russian composer and music director, commissions Benjamin Britten to compose an opera, **Peter Grimes**.

Enid Blyton publishes **Five on a Treasure Island,** the first book of her **The Famous Five** Series.

1943:

In April the Ministry of Information release a film **Desert Victory** which goes on to win this year's Academy Award for Best Documentary Feature.

Three pigeons, 'White Vision', 'Winkie' and 'Tyke' become the first recipients of the **Dickin Medal,** an award for any animal displaying conspicuous gallantry and devotion to duty whilst serving with the armed forces or civil emergency forces.

1944:

The prohibition of married women working as teachers is lifted.

Laurence Olivier's **Henry V** is released. It is the first of Shakespeare's works to be filmed in colour.

A Child of Our Time by Michael Tippett has its first performances at the Adelphi Theatre.

Bing Crosby was 'big' in Britain and his **Swinging on a Star** from the film, **Going My Way** won the Oscar for best original song.

On the BBC wireless, **Much Binding in the Marsh** and **Variety Bandbox** make their debut.

1945:

The **BBC Light Programme** is launched, concentrating on broadcasting mainstream light music and entertainment.

Giles first appears in the Sunday Express; George Orwell's **Animal Farm** is published and Noël Coward's film **Brief Encounter** starring Celia Johnson and Trevor Howard is released.

The first of the **Poldark** novels by Winston Graham is published, **Ross Poldark.**

1946:

The American dance craze, the **Jitterbug** invades Britain.

The Royal Opera House in Covent Garden re-opens after the War with the Royal Ballet performing **The Sleeping Beauty.**

BBC radio debuts include **American Letter** by Alistair Cooke, **Woman's Hour** and **Dick Barton Special Agent**. BBC television is resumed.

The first post-war **FA Cup Final** is held at Wembley and Derby County beat Charlton Athletic.

1947:

Ealing Studios release their first Ealing Comedy, **Hue and Cry**.

Compton Mackenzie's comic novel **Whisky Galore** is published.

The first soft **toilet paper** goes on sale in the UK, at Harrods.

Conductor Malcolm Sargent is knighted for his services to music and Lizbeth Webb has a hit with **This is My Lovely Day** from the film **Bless the Bride.**

1948:

BBC radio debuts include **Take it From Here** and **Any Questions?**

The first open-air museum in Britain, the **Welsh Folk Museum** opens at St Fagans.

The first new comprehensive schools open in Potters Bar and Hillingdon.

The '**Black Widow'** road safety poster – 'Keep death off the road, Carelessness kills' is issued.

1949:

Book at Bedtime debuts on BBC radio,

Laurence Olivier's film **Hamlet** becomes the first British film to win an Oscar for 'Best Picture' and **The Third Man** is released.

Nineteen Eighty-Four by George Orwell is published and Enid Blyton introduces Noddy in **Little Noddy Goes to Toyland** and **The Secret Seven.**

Science

A Decade of Inventions

In the 1940s, research for and by the military played a significant part in all new developments. The atom bomb has influenced the world ever since, but there were many other inventions in the 1940s as well. Antibiotic penicillin; the insecticide DDT; synthetic rubber; kidney dialyses machines; the Jeep; Tupperware and duct tape. New technologies included radar, the jet engine, the Colossus electronic computer, and the first commercial flights with pressurised cabins were inaugurated.

The Aerosol Can

The concept of an aerosol originated as early as 1790 in France and in 1837 a soda siphon incorporating a valve was invented.

Metal spray cans were tested as early as 1862 but constructed from heavy steel they were too bulky to be commercially successful. In 1927, a Norwegian engineer patented the first aerosol can and valve that could hold and dispense products and propellant systems.

However, it was during the war that the US government funded research into a portable way for servicemen to spray malaria-carrying bugs and two department of Agriculture researchers developed a small aerosol can pressurised by a liquefied fluorocarbon.

America also developed a lightweight aluminium can, making a cheap and practical way to dispense hair spray, foams, powders and creams and when spray paint was invented in 1949, provided graffiti artists with the tools of their trade.

Velcro

Although Velcro was not released to the world until 1955, it all started in 1941 when George de Mestral, a Swiss inventor, took his dog for a walk in the woods. When he got home, he noticed that burrs from the burdock plant had attached themselves to the dog's fur and to his trousers.

Being a curious man, he examined the burrs under a microscope and saw that the tips of the burr contained tiny hooks that attached themselves to the fibres in his trousers. He spent the next 14 years trying to duplicate this system of 'hook and eye' fastener.

1/2" WIDE
Velcro® Brand Tape Strips - Hook, Black
Strong acrylic adhesive can be used outdoors/indoor

Made of heat-treated nylon, with 300 hooks per square inch, Velcro is now found everywhere, blood pressure cuffs, orthopaedic devices, clothing and footwear, sporting and camping equipment, toys and recreation, airline seat cushions and Velcro was used in the first human artificial heart transplant to hold parts together.

Duct Tape

During the war, cartridges used for grenade launchers came boxed, sealed with wax and taped over to protect them from moisture. American soldiers needed to spend precious minutes, in the heat of battle, to open them.

Vesta Stoudt was working in a factory packing these cartridges and thought there must be an easier way. She came up with the idea of a tape made from strong, water-proof fabric. Her company not being interested, she wrote directly to the President who luckily passed on her proposal to the military.

Johnson & Johnson was assigned to develop the tape which now comprises a piece of mesh cloth and a pressure-sensitive adhesive. The original green sticky cloth became known as 'duck tape' to the troops and now, is used to make repairs from boots to furniture, in motorsports to patch up dents, by film crews who have a version called gaffer's tape, and even astronauts pack a roll when they go into space.

M&Ms

'The milk chocolate melts in your mouth, not in your hand' and the origins of M&Ms date back to the 1930s.

During the Spanish Civil War, American candy manufacturer, Forrest Mars, saw British soldiers eating Smarties - the sugar-coated chocolate beans that Rowntrees had begun making in 1882.

The sweets were popular with soldiers because they were less messy than pure chocolate. Forest Mars patented M&Ms in 1941, originally in cardboard tubes, but by 1948 the packaging changed to a plastic pouch.

LPs

In 1948, Columbia Records held a press conference at the Waldorf-Astoria Hotel in New York City to unveil their new technology, which was a non-breakable, 12-inch, microgroove disc that had a playing time of twenty-three minutes per side. Six times as much music as previous records and the start of the modern recording industry.

1950:

Feb: Clement Attlee wins the General Election for Labour giving them a 2nd term in government after their triumph in 1945.

Aug: 4,000 British troops are sent to Korea.

1951:

May: 3 George VI opens the Festival of Britain in London, including the Royal Festival Hall, Dome of Discovery and Skylon.

Oct: The Conservative Party led by Winston Churchill wins the General Election. It is six years since he was previously Prime Minister.

1952:

Feb: King George VI dies at Sandringham House, aged 56. He is succeeded by his daughter, Princess Elizabeth.

Dec: 4–9 The Great Smog blankets London, causing transport chaos and, it is believed, around 4,000 deaths.

1953:

Jan: Dwight D Eisenhower is sworn in as the 34th President of the United States.

Jan: Devastating North Sea Floods.

Jun: The coronation of Queen Elizabeth II takes place at Westminster Abbey. A public holiday is declared.

1954:

May: Roger Bannister becomes the first person to break the four-minute-mile at Oxford

Jul: Nearly a decade after the end of WW2, food rationing in the UK ends, with the lifting of restrictions on sale and purchase of meat.

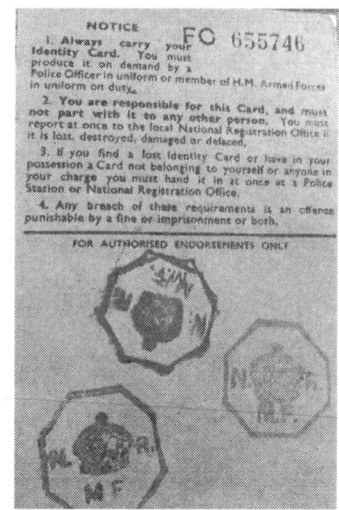

1952: In February, compulsory Identity Cards are abolished. Brought in under the National Registration Act of 1939, every person, including children, had to carry it at all times, to show who they were and where they lived.

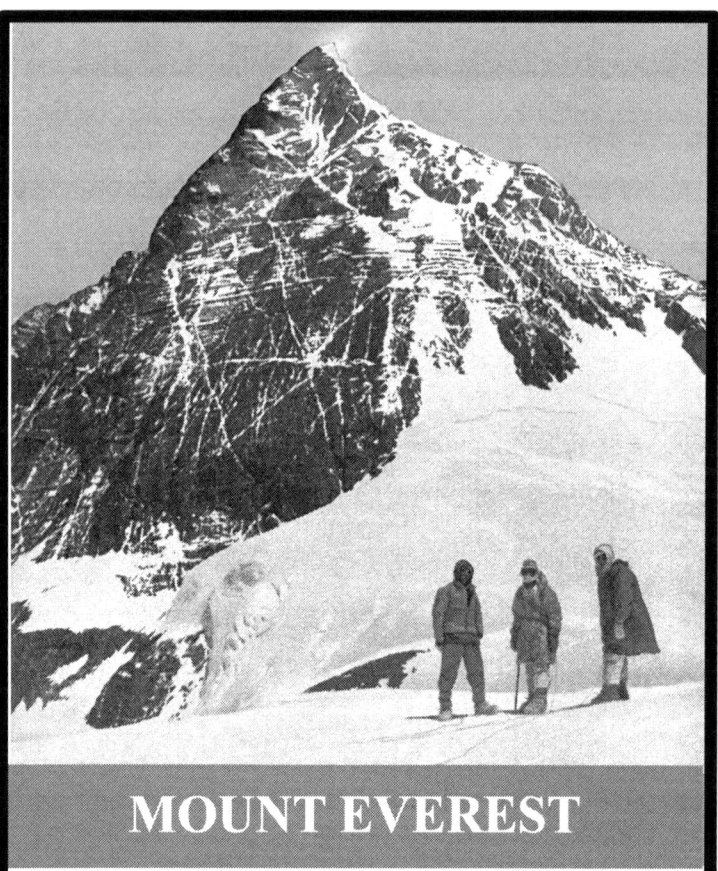

MOUNT EVEREST

1953: On 29th May: Emund Hillary and Tenzing Norgay become the first men to reach the summit of Mount Everest. The British Expedition was led by Col. John Hunt and the news reached England on Coronation Day.

1955:

Apr: Winston Churchill resigns as Prime Minister due to ill-health and the Foreign Secretary, Anthony Eden, succeeds him.

Sep: ITV broadcasts the UK's first commercial television ending the BBC's 18-year monopoly. The first advertisement shown is for Gibbs SR toothpaste.

1956:

Feb: British spies, Guy Burgess and Donald Maclean show up in the Soviet Union after being missing for 5 years.

Apr: British MI6 diver Lionel Crabb, dives into Portsmouth Harbour to investigate a visiting Soviet cruiser and vanishes.

Jul: Gamal Abdel Nasser, the Egyptian leader, announces the nationalisation of the Suez Canal, beginning the Suez Crisis.

1957:

Jan: Anthony Eden resigns as Prime Minister due to ill health and Harold Macmillan succeeds him.

Mar: Egypt re-opens the Suez Canal and petrol rationing ends in May.

Jun: ERNIE selects the first Premium Bond winners.

1958:

Feb: The Manchester United FC team plane crashes at Munich Airport. 7 of the players are killed and an 8th dies later in hospital.

Jun: The Queen officially reopens Gatwick Airport which has been expanded at a cost of more than £7,000,000.

1959:

Jun: Christopher Cockerell's 'Hovercraft' is officially launched

Jul: UK Postcodes are introduced for the first time, in Norwich.

1956 Oct: The Queen switched on the world's first nuclear powered electricity generating station at Calder Hall, Cumberland. It was a fantastic engineering achievement, built within three years of cutting the first sod on the south side of the river Calder.

1958: In June, the first parking meter in Britain was installed in Grosvenor Square, near the US Embassy in Westminster. Parking for one hour cost six shillings (30p) and those who overstayed or neglected to pay at all received a £2 penalty.

THE HOME

During the early 50's, very few people had a television and the wireless reigned supreme. Daytime programmes were for wives, mothers and their children. 'Workers Playtime' continued to "come to you from a factory somewhere in England" and singers were interspersed with the major comedians of the day, Arthur Askey, Tommy Trinder, Charlie Chester and Ted Ray.

Music was important, with 'Music while you work' and 'Housewives Choice'. Soap operas gripped us, 'Mrs Dale's Diary' and 'The Archers'. Sunday lunchtimes meant 'Two-Way Family Favourites', music and messages for the troops in Germany. In the evening we could "Stop the roar of London's mighty traffic" and listen to 'In Town Tonight', and the children weren't forgotten, they had 'Listen with Mother', Children's Hour 'Children's Favourites' with Uncle Mac.

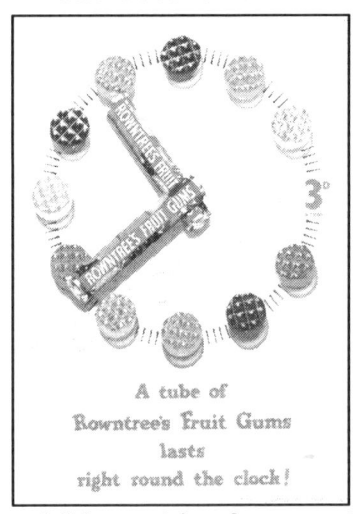

In 1958, Rowntree brought out their television advertisement, "Don't Forget the Fruit Gums Mum"

A tube of Rowntree's Fruit Gums lasts right round the clock!

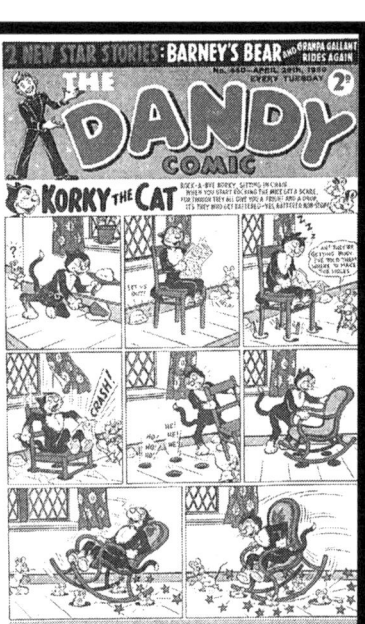

Sweets were rationed until 1953 but children with a few pennies pocket money could choose sweeties from the rows of jars on the shelves. Four blackjacks or fruit salads for a penny, a Barratt's Sherbet Fountain with a stick of liquorice in it, raspberry drops, dolly mixture or toffees. You could 'smoke' a sweet cigarette whilst reading Dan Dare's adventures in Eagle or laugh with Radio Fun, Beano and Dandy comics.

The drabness of the war years gave way by the mid '50s to an age of colour and plastic in the home. Textile restrictions had been lifted and consumers were eager for new brightly patterned curtains and upholstery, but it was the kitchen that was changed most, with the introductionsof coloured plastic goods.

The concept of 'built in' wall units and cupboards, rather than free standing wooden units appeared but it was only when stores such as MFI appeared that fitted kitchens become affordable for most.

In 1952 the nuclear family was the norm, father out at work and mother busy with the housework. Less than 10% of households had a refrigerator, meat was stored in a wire mesh 'safe' in the larder, vegetables wilted on a rack and shopping was done daily. It was the time of spam fritters, salmon sandwiches, tinned fruit with evaporated milk and ham salad for high tea on Sundays. Salad in the summer consisted of round lettuce, cucumber and tomatoes, and the only dressing available was Heinz Salad Cream, olive oil only came in tiny bottles from the chemist for your ears!

Many housewifes wanted a Kenwood Chef to make baking and food preparation easier. And these new domestic inventions coincided with an upsurge in 'do-it-yourself' or DIY from the mid-1950s. The nation that had adopted a 'make do and mend' attitude during wartime privations took very readily to the idea of improving their homes themselves.

1950 'Painting by numbers' kits are first marketed by the Palmer Show Card Paint Company in Detroit.

The Festival Ballet, founded by Alicia Markova and Anton Dolin makes its debut performance.

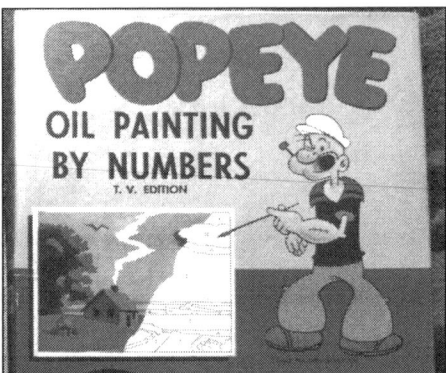

1951 Dennis the Menace makes his first appearance in The Beano comic.

The first ever Miss World beauty pageant is held as part of the Festival of Britain.

1952 The first TV detector van begins clamping down on the estimated 150,000 British households that watch television without a licence.

Vladimir Tretchikoff paints his best-selling work, 'Chinese Girl' sometimes known as 'The Green Lady'

'The Mousetrap' by Agatha Christie opens at the New Ambassadors Theatre.

1953 The current affairs series Panorama is first shown on BBC.

The 'Piltdown Man' is exposed as a hoax.

'The Moka', the first Italian espresso coffee bar is the first to open in London and Laura Ashley sells her first printed fabrics.

1954 Two months after the author's death, Richard Burton makes famous his 'First Voice' in Dylan Thomas's radio play, 'Under Milk Wood'.

'The Fellowship of the Ring', the first of three volumes of J.R.R. Tolkien's epic fantasy novel, 'The Lord of the Rings' is published.

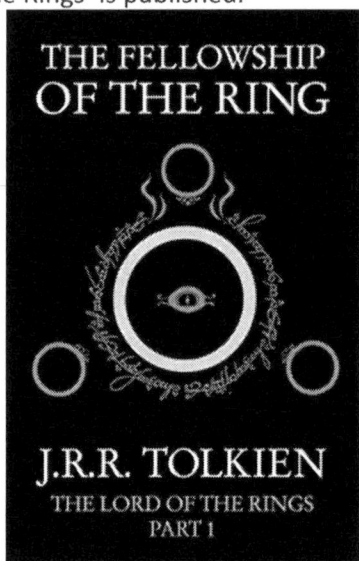

1955 Pietro Annigoni's iconic portrait of the Queen is unveiled.

The 'Guinness Book of Records' is first published.

1956 Harold Macmillan, Chancellor of the Exchequer, announces the launch of Premium Bonds with a top prize of £1,000.

The Queen awards Ninette de Valois's ballet school and companies the title "Royal" and they become the Royal Ballet of England.

1957 The cartoon character, Andy Capp first appears in northern editions of the 'Daily Mirror'.

The Queen broadcasts her first Royal Christmas Message on television.

1958 The first Duke of Edinburgh Award is presented at Buckingham Palace.

The practice of presenting debutantes to the royal court is abolished.

Both 'Grandstand' and 'Blue Peter' make their debut on BBC television.

1959 The ballerina, Margot Fonteyn is released from prison in Panama, having been suspected of being involved in a coup against the government.

BBC airs 'Juke Box Jury' chaired by David Jacobs, for the first time.

SHE SAT DOWN ON A LITTLE BOULDER AND THEN BERTIE GOT 'A LITTLE BOLDER' TOO

1954, Donald McGill, the English graphic artist who painted and popularised 'saucy seaside postcards' was found guilty in Lincoln, of breaching the Obscene Publications Act of 1857. He was fined £50 with £25 costs.

The scenes he painted were most often at the seaside and featured an array of buxom young women, fat old ladies, drunken men, honeymoon couples and vicars, all displaying a fine level of social commentary and a 'naughty' sense of humour.

"I'm in a ticklish position here!"

FESTIVAL OF BRITAIN

1951

In 1951, the government took inspiration from the Great Exhibition of 1851, to organise the 'Festival of Britain' with the aim of promoting a feeling of recovery in the still war damaged country. Sited on the South Bank in London, the exhibits were to celebrate British industry, arts and science and led by a young architect, Hugh Casson, the buildings themselves turned out to be just as important and inspiring.

- The largest dome in the world at the time, standing 93ft tall with a diameter of 365ft which held exhibitions on the theme of discovery, the New World, the Polar regions, the Sea, the Sky and Outer Space.

- Adjacent to the Dome was the Skylon, a stunning, futuristic-looking structure, it was a vertical cigar shaped tower supported by cables that gave it the impression of floating above the ground.

- The Telekinema was a 400-seat, state-of-the-art, cinema which had the necessary technology to screen both films and large screen television and proved to be one of the most popular attractions.

Also built were the Royal Festival Hall and a new wing of the Science Museum whilst upriver from the main site was Battersea Park, home to the Festival fun-fair, pleasure gardens, rides and open-air amusements.

1950 The black and white film, **All the King's Men** picked up the Oscar for Best Picture of the year. Based on the Pulitzer Prize winning book by Robert Penn Warren, it relates the rise and fall of an ambitious and ruthless politician, Willie Stark, during the depression in the American South.

1951 **All About Eve** starred Bette Davis and Anne Baxter and received a record 14 Academy Award nominations – four of them for the female acting - and won six, including Best Picture. It also featured Marilyn Monroe in one of her earliest roles

1952 Gene Kelly and Leslie Caron in her acting debut, had a huge success with **An American in Paris**. The climax of the film is a 17-minute ballet danced by the pair causing controversy over part of Caron's dance sequence with a chair. The censor called it 'sexually provocative' to which, surprised, Caron answered, *"What can you do with a chair?"*

1953 **The Greatest Show on Earth** set in the Ringling Bros. and Barnum and Bailey Circus was certainly a great show. The circus troupe, 1,400 people appear, plus hundreds of animals and 60 railroad cars of equipment and tents. The actors learned their respective circus roles and participated in the acts.

1954 This year, the trials and tribulations of three US Army soldiers and their women in Hawaii during the lead up to the attack on Pearl Harbour won **From Here to Eternity** the accolades.

1955 **The Seven Year Itch** premièred and contains the famous image of Marilyn Monroe standing on a subway grate as her white dress is blown upwards by a passing train. **On the Waterfront** won the Oscar.

1956 The first and only entirely British film to have won the Oscar for Best Picture by this time was **Hamlet** starring Laurence Oliver in 1948 and the prize was not picked up again until **Tom Jones** in 1963.
An American romantic drama **Marty** was this year's winner and enjoyed international success, winning the Palme d'Or also.

1957 **Around the World in 80 days** was the first film to win Best Picture when all its fellow nominees were also filmed in colour.

1958 British director, David Lean's epic war film **The Bridge on the River Kwai** won the Academy Award for Best Picture. British actor Alec Guinness starred, and it became the highest earning film of the year.

1959 Leslie Caron was **Gigi** and the film won all nine of its Oscar nominations. The screenplay, songs and lyrics were written by Alan Jay Lerner and music by Frederick Loewe was arranged by André Previn.

British Film in the 1950s

If the 1940s was seen by many as 'the golden age' of British cinema, it was followed in the 50's by 'the dark age'. The two major cinema chains, Rank and Associated British Pictures embarked on a programme of cinema closures and admissions dropped by 500m over the ten years.

Even though no Oscars were won, there were good films: The most popular genre was the British war film. **The Cruel Sea, The Dam Busters, Reach for the Sky** and **Sink the Bismarck!** were top box-office attractions, while **The Bridge on the River Kwai** was the British cinema's biggest international success of the decade.

Some criticised the nostalgia but there were some changes to the traditional formula of male, stiff upper lip heroics, **A Town Like Alice** was shown from the female point of view and **Ice Cold in Alex** has an assertive female lead, the nurse who sorely tempts the neurotic British officer 'hero'..

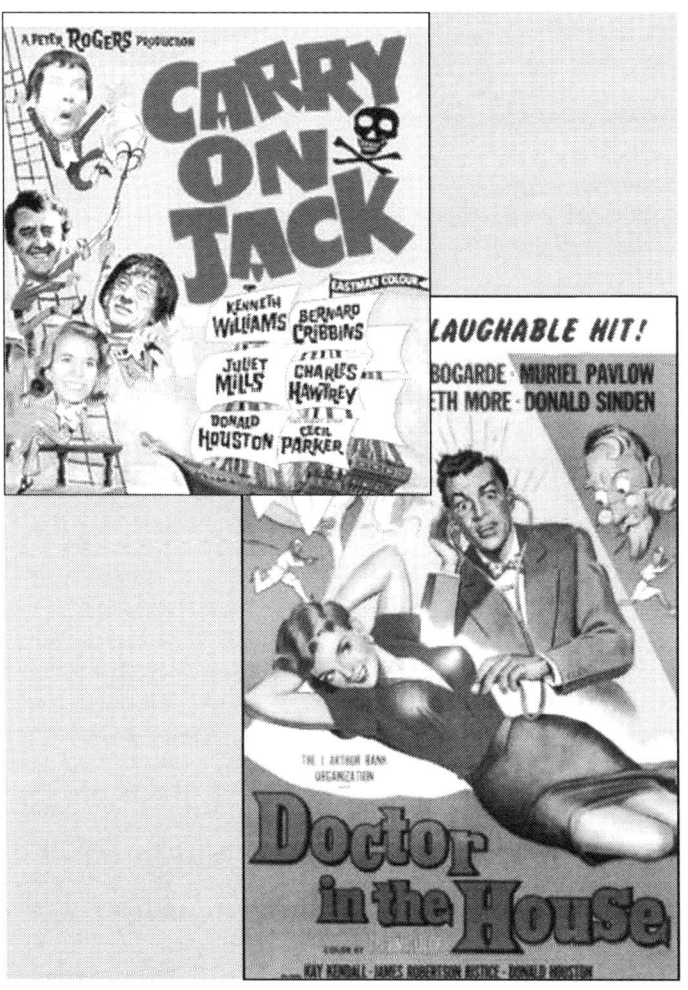

Comedy was always popular. Ealing Studios produced **The Lavender Hill Mob**, **The Man in the White Suit** and **The Ladykillers** all featuring Britain's finest actor-star of the time, Alec Guinness. When Ealing closed in 1958, their gentle comedy was replaced by the raunchy high spirits of the **Carry On** films, peaking with **Carry On Nurse**.

The **St Trinian's** films had their following, as did the **Doctor** series, launched with spectacular success by **Doctor in the House**. **I'm All Right Jack** was a satire on industrial relations and **The Curse of Frankenstein** was famously described by the critic for the Observer newspaper as being amongst the most repulsive films she had ever seen. Quite a contrast to **Genevieve** and the London to Brighton car race.

At the end of the 50s, **Room at the Top** was a huge international success, and its sexual frankness and Northern realism ushered in a new era.

AFTER THE WAR
THE 'NEW LOOK'

As the decade began, the simple, drab, styles from wartime remained as materials were still in short supply and for many this remained the case for several years. However, with the introduction of colour into the country again, in the home and in textiles, fashion for many women returned with a vengeance. The years are known for two silhouettes, that of Christian Dior's 'New Look', the tiny waist, pointy breasts and a full skirt to just below the knee, all achieved with a "waspie" girdle and the pointiest bra seen in history and the pencil slim tubular skirt, also placing emphasis on a narrow waist.

Neat, tailored suits with pencil skirts or fitted dresses, now updated with block colours were the choice for work and by the second half of the decade, the wide circle skirts in colourful cotton prints were in and were worn supported by bouffant net petticoats, stiffened either with conventional starch or a strong sugar solution, to give the right look.

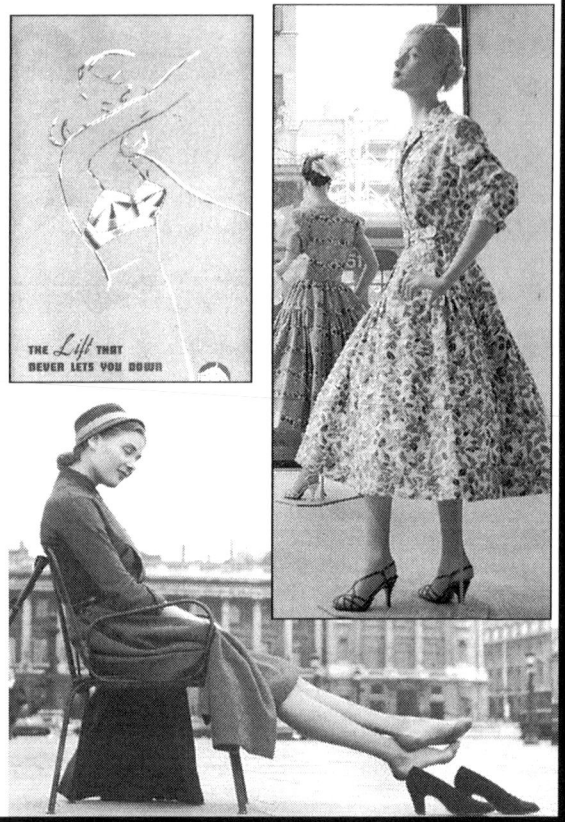

THE *Lift* THAT NEVER LETS YOU DOWN

Elizabeth Taylor

ALL CHANGE

If a lady was 'formally dressed', she would wear short white cotton gloves for daytime and a decorative hat as a finishing touch. Hairstyles 'for the lady' were stiff, structured and arranged even when worn loose. The permanent wave, in styles worn by the Queen and Elizabeth Taylor, were universally worn, the styling more easily copied with the introduction of hair lacquers and plastic rollers. By 1955 almost 30,000 hair salons had sprung up in Britain.

Grace Kelly epitomised the elegance of the 50s, but there were many who rebelled against the look, including actress Audrey Hepburn who often wore simple black sweaters, flat shoes and short. They gave a continental, chic alternative and had many followers. In 1954, Chanel began to produce boxy classic Chanel suit jackets and slim skirts in braid trimmed, highly textured tweeds. The lines were straight down, losing the nipped in waist and this fashion was easy to copy by major chain stores and very wearable.

THE YOUNG ONES

It was different, the new 'teenager' had their own ideas, girls sported youthful ponytails and were no longer prepared to look like their mothers until they were of age.

The consumer boom arrived with 'teen' clothes becoming available and fashion was influenced by America. Rock 'n' roll idols and film stars set fashions and many boys wanted the black leather and denim jeans look from Brando whilst girls embraced the 'preppie' full dirndl skirts teamed with a scoop neck blouse, back to front cardigan or tight polo neck.

There were the Teddy Boys and Beatniks, but the majority of British male teenagers looked smart. A basic blazer or jacket, with a fashionable narrow tie and even suede shoes.

WEDDING DRESS OF THE DECADE

Grace Kelly and Prince Rainier of Monaco married in 1956. Her dress was designed by Helen Rose, an American who spent the bulk of her career with MGM and was a wedding present from the film studio. It was made from 25 yards of silk taffeta and used antique rose-point lace and pearls.

The fitted bodice was overlaid with lace to the throat, culminating in a small standing collar and closed with a long centre row of tiny buttons. The long sleeves were also lace, and the dress had a full skirt and sweeping train.

The romantic look was completed by the lace and pearl encrusted prayer book the bride carried down the aisle.

WINNING THE POOLS

Football Pools were a 'betting pool' for predicting the outcome of top-level football matches taking place in the coming week. It was typically cheap to play and entries were sent to Littlewoods or Vernons, by post, or collected from your home by agents.

The most popular game was the Treble Chance where you had to predict the matches to end in a 'draw'.

O TWO RESULTS FROM EACH RULED SECTION			CORRECT SCOR DOUBLES · TREBLES · ACCUMULATI						
180-1 TEN RESULTS									
				Home	Away	H	A	H	A
South'pton Bury				Sheff. Un.	Ipswich T.				
Peterboro' Barnsley				Grimsby T.	Scunthorpe				
Aldershot Southport				Leeds U.	Sunderland				
Bradford C. Barrow				Swansea	Stoke C.				
Brentford Mansfield				Bristol R.	Crystal P.				
Crewe Al. Gillingham				Notts C.	Bournem'th				
York C. Doncaster				Max.: Doubles £1, Trebles & Accum. 5/-, Min. 3d					
Dunf'mline Raith R.				**SHORT LIST**					
Dundee Dundee U.				**11-1 THREE HOMES**		**12-1 THREE AWAYS**			
Rangers Hibernian									
Bolton W. Fulham				W. Brom. Burnley					
Everton Sheff. W.				West Ham Tottenh'm					
Leicester Notts F.				Derby Co. Cardiff C					
Chelsea Charlton				Leeds Un. Sunderl'd					
Brighton Hull City				Notts Co. Bourne'th					
Colchester Coventry				Shrewsb'y Bristol C					
Millwall Watford				Airdrie Kilmarn'k					
Chesterf'ld Exeter C.				Falkirk Motherw'l					
Oxford U. Hartlepools				**STAKES**					
Torquay U. Lincoln C.									
Arsenal Man. Un.				**TREBLE**					
Birm'ngh'm Leyton O.				**12-1 THREE WINS**		**20-1 TWO WINS ONE DRAW**			
Blackburn Liverpool									
Blackpool Wolves				W. Brom. Burnley					
Man. City Aston Villa				Notts Co. Bourne'th					
Luton T. Rotherham				Shrewsb'y Bristol C					
Middlesbro' Huddersf'd									
Newcastle Portsmouth									
Walsall Preston									

Britain was almost obsessed with all things American after the war and the first Wimpy Bars opened in Britain in 1954, selling hamburgers, expresso coffee and milkshakes. Named after a fat friend of 'Popeye', the Wimpy bar added the 'British' elements of waitress service and cutlery. They became very popular, especially with the decade's 'new' teenagers who welcomed the addition to the high street's coffee bars and juke boxes.

CAN YOU COME OUT TO PLAY?

Friends would knock on the door straight after breakfast and you would often not come back till tea-time. Streets had little traffic and could be transformed with a couple of pullovers into a football or cricket pitch.

Towns had areas still devastated by bomb damage providing excellent dens and in the country, you could 'go up the woods', ideal for Cowboys and Indians. Those with bikes would cycle for miles, heading for the countryside or city parks to find trees to climb and fall out of, knees always seemed to be grazed and muddy. There were streams to paddle in or fish for stickle backs.

Girls could spend hours skipping or playing hopscotch drawn on the path, whilst their 'babies' slept in the toy prams alongside. Boys playing British bulldog would be rushing past girls, their dresses tucked into the legs of their knickers, practicing handstands against a wall or cartwheels. Saturday night was bath night!

BUTLIN'S HOLIDAY CAMP SKEGNESS
IT'S QUICKER BY RAIL

THE GREAT BRITISH SEASIDE HOLIDAY

The heyday of the great British seaside holiday was in the 1950s and particularly for those living in industrial towns where 'wakes weeks', when the whole factory would shut down and all workers took their annual two weeks holiday at the same time. Convoys of coaches would leave the grime behind, ferrying happy families to the seaside. Blackpool or Scarborough, Brighton or Margate.

The choice was to stay in a guest house or hotel, or for thousands, it was the excitement of a holiday camp such as Butlins or . Heaven for children, the many activities on offer included the swimming pool, cinema, fairground rides all 'inclusive', no extra charge. Three meals a day were included, served in the communal dining hall and 'Red Coats' at Butlins, or 'Blue Coats' at Pontins, organised daytime activities for both adults and children. Even a 'knobbly knees' and 'glamorous granny' contests. For the evenings, there was the traditional entertainment, song and dance and comedy shows.

The British seaside resorts provided fun and respite from daily life for the masses, with amusement arcades, candyfloss stalls and seafood shacks selling cockles and whelks in paper cones. Cafes served fish and chips with white bread and butter, accompanied by mugs of tea. There were donkey rides on the sand, roundabouts, helter-skelters and dodgems. On the prom shops sold rock, postcards, buckets and spades and, whatever the weather, families in rented deck chairs sheltered behind windbreaks on the beach, watching the children build sandcastles, play ball and paddle in the sea.

Only the unpredictable British weather could spoil the fun.

1950 The UK singles chart did not exist before 1952 and a song's popularity was measured by the sales of sheet music. This year's top sellers ranged from **You're Breaking My Heart** by Vic Damone, through **Bewitched** by Doris Day to **Rudolph the Red Nosed Reindeer**, the Christmas 'no 1' from Bing Crosby.

1951 **I Taut I Saw a Puddy Tat** was sung by Mel Blanc who was 'the voice' of Tweety and Silvester in the US cartoons. It was the best seller for three weeks, sold over 2m copies and has been recorded by several artists since. Less of a novelty, was **Too Young** by Jimmy Young, who went on to DJ for Radio 2 for almost 30 years.

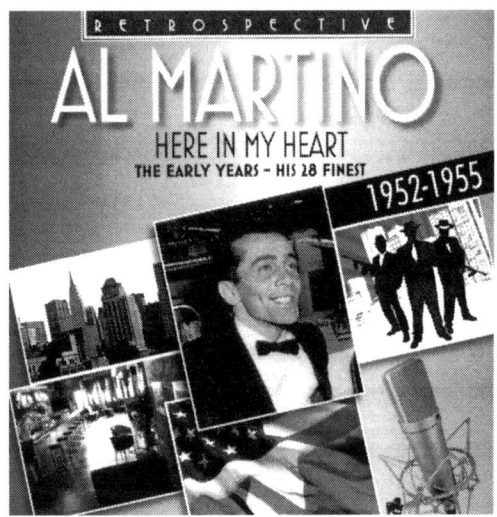

1952 The first 'official' No 1 in the UK, compiled from the best-selling songs by a telephone sample of about 20 shops and published in 'NME' in November was **Here in My Heart** by Al Martino.

1953 Frankie Lane was the singer of the year, **I Believe** topped the charts for 18 non-consecutive weeks and he had 8 top 10 entries, with 2 reaching No 1. Both David Whitfield and Frankie Lane reached a joint top spot, with the same song, at the same time **Answer Me.**

1954 **Secret Love** was Doris Day's second No1 and became the best-selling record of the year. Eddie Calvert, the British trumpeter had a No 1 for 9 weeks, with **Oh Mein Papa**.

1955 Songs seemed to stay at the top longer in the 50's, and Slim Whitmans **Rose Marie** from the musical of the same name, was there for 9 weeks. Tony Bennett made another song from a show, **Stranger in Paradise** from Kismet, a hit too. year but the best-seller was **I'll Be Home** by Pat Boone.

1956 Now, Rock 'n' Roll hit the world! Bill Hayley & his Comets, stormed to No 1 with **Rock Around the Clock** right at the beginning of the year but the best-seller was **I'll Be Home** by Pat Boone.

1957 This was a year for the Brits with hits from Tommy Steele **Singing the Blues**, Frankie Vaughan's **Garden of Eden**, Lonnie Donegan with **Cumberland Gap** and **Gamblin' Man** but the Canadian Paul Anka outsold them with **Diana**.

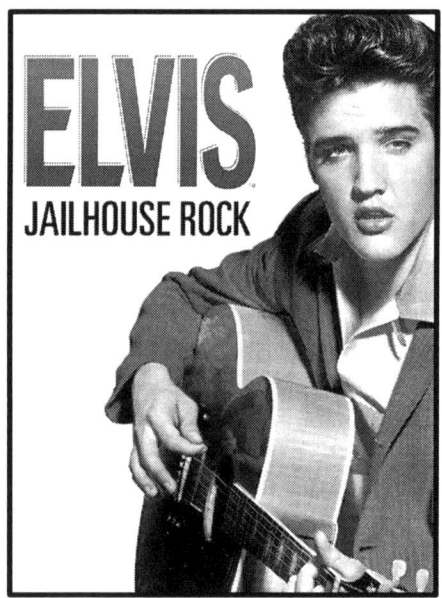

1958 Elvis Presley continued on his way to 21 UK No 1's with **Jailhouse Rock** and the Everly Brothers had the first of their No 1's with **All I Have to Do Is Dream.**

1959 **Living Doll** by Cliff Richard and the Drifters made it to No 1 and later with The Shadows with **Travelling Light**. Adam Faith makes his debut with **What Do You Want**.

IN THE 1950s

BUDDY HOLLY

During his short career, Holly wrote and recorded many songs. He is often regarded as the artist who defined the traditional rock-and-roll lineup of two guitars, bass, and drums.

That'll Be The Day topped the US "Best Sellers in Stores" chart in September 1957 when they also released **Peggy Sue.**

Buddy Holly (above) and Buddy Holly and the Crickets.(left)

The 50's legend had a huge posthumous hit with **It Doesn't Matter Anymore** and **Raining in My Heart** in 1959, shortly after he was tragically killed in a plane crash in the February. His death was the event later dubbed as "The Day the Music Died" by singer-songwriter Don McLean in his 1971 song **American Pie.**

BRITISH ROCK AND ROLL

In the '50s, American rock 'n' roll arrived in Britain, dominated the popular music world and became a huge influence on the newly burgeoning youth culture.

It was a fusion of rhythm and blues, gospel music, country and western and pop. Bill Hayley's '**Rock Around the Clock**', Elvis with '**Hound Dog**' and '**Jailhouse Rock**', Little Richard and Jerry Lee Lewis, inspired British the rock'n'roll groups who emerged from the already popular skiffle groups.

Tommy Steele was one of the first to become a teen idol, with Marty Wilde, Billy Fury and others soon following, but it was Cliff Richard and The Shadows' hit '**Move It**', in 1958, that caused British rock 'n' roll to explode.

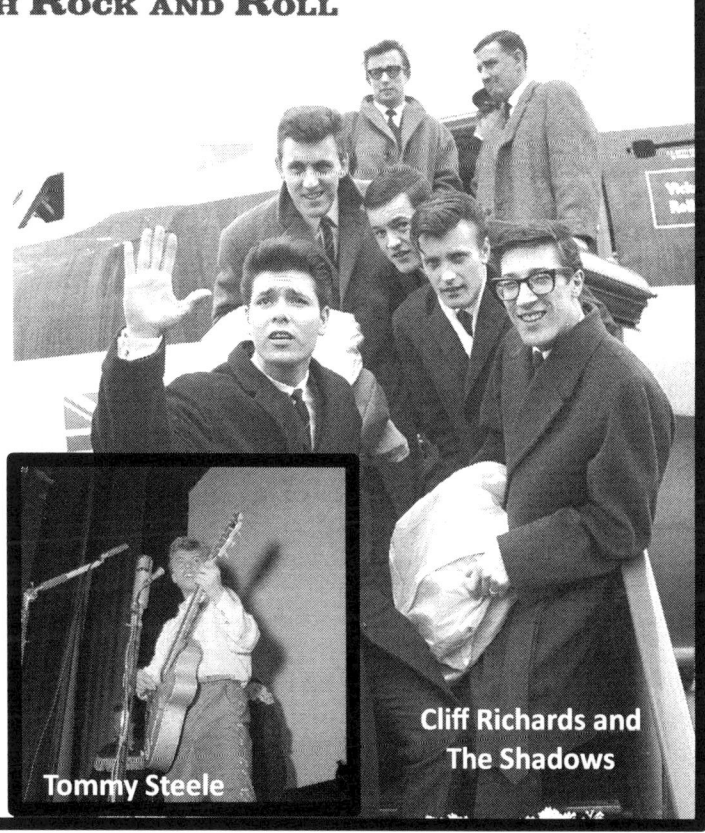

Tommy Steele

Cliff Richards and The Shadows

SCIENCE AND NATURE

A DECADE OF INVENTIONS

The 1950s was a period when a plethora of new innovations and inventions were made many still very much in use in the 21st Century. Credit cards, super glue, video tape recorder, oral contraceptives, non-stick Teflon pans, hovercraft, integrating circuit, microchip, transistor radio, heart pacemaker, wireless tv remote, solar panels, polio vaccine, automatic sliding doors, polypropylene, Fortran, the hard disk, power steering and of course, the hula hoop and Barbie dolls.

Black Box Flight Recorder

This invention by an Australian, David Warren, has saved many lives since it was introduced in 1953.

Before then, the cause of most plane crashes, unless there was a surviving pilot, remained unknown, and working as a researcher at an Aeronautical Laboratory in Melbourne, Warren realised that if there was a device in the cockpit that recorded the pilot's voice and read instruments, the information gathered could reveal the cause of the crash and could possibly prevent subsequent ones.

His first device called the Flight Memory Unit could record about four hours of voice and certain parameters but was rejected on grounds of privacy by the Australian aviation community.

Luckily, British officials accepted it, production of the devices in fireproof containers, began and it was taken up by airlines around the world. Some years later it was made compulsory for Australia.

Bar Codes

Joseph Woodland and Bernard Silver invented the first bar code in 1951. At the time Bernard was a graduate at Drexel Institute of Technology, Philadelphia which was contacted by a local food store that wanted a means to automatically read product information when customers checked out.

Woodland was at the beach thinking about this when he started drawing random lines in the sand with four of his fingers. He realised he had found one way to solve the food store owner's problem, data could be represented by varying the widths and spacings of parallel lines and thus be able to be read by a machine.

Using UV light sensitive ink he and his colleagues worked on prototypes until they came out with the scannable bar code which has helped make the modern economy.

Winter of Terror

The Winter of Terror was a three-month period during the winter of 1950–1951 when the Alps were hit by the worst avalanche season ever seen. Thought to be the result of an Atlantic warm front meeting a polar cold front, the destruction mostly affected Austria and Switzerland.

A January snowstorm that lasted two days, added up to four metres of snowfall to a base that was already twice the seasonal average and strong winds caused drifting which led to unstable masses of snow being built up over wide areas. This was to come tumbling down in hundreds of avalanches, burying villages and killing in excess of 200 people.

Thousands of acres of valuable forest were damaged, livestock suffocated, and hundreds of buildings were destroyed. The Swiss town of Andermatt was hit by six avalanches within an hour and 13 people died.

Fifties Floods

1952: In August, the tiny village of Lynmouth, north Devon, suffered the worst river flood in English history. On the 15th, just over 9in (230mm) of rain fell, estimated at 90m tons, over north Devon and west Somerset.

The 1953 Floods in the Netherlands

1953: The great North Sea flood of January caused catastrophic damage and loss of life in Scotland, England, Belgium and The Netherlands and was Britain's worst peacetime disaster on record claiming the lives of 307 people.

In the Netherlands where 50% of the land is less than 1 metre (3.3 ft) above sea level there were 1,836 deaths and widespread damage

1950 The 4th **FIFA World Cup** is held for the first time since 1938 (1942 and 1946 were cancelled during the war). Brazil is the host nation and loses to Uruguay in the finals.

American Joey Maxim wins the light-heavyweight world **Boxing** title, stopping World Champion Freddie Mills of Britain in 10 rounds.

The 4th **British Empire Games** (later called the Commonwealth Games) are held in New Zealand.

1951 Ben Hogan wins the **Masters Tournament** for his 5th major title. He goes on to win the **US Open** title later in the year.

In **First Division football**, Tottenham Hotspur win the 1950/51 title and in the **FA Cup**, Newcastle United beats Blackpool.

1952 At the summer **Olympics** in Helsinki, Finland, Emil Zátopek of Czechoslovakia wins three gold medals. The 5,000m and 10,000m and the third - he decided at the last minute to compete in the first marathon of his life. He was nicknamed the 'Czech Locomotive'.

Rocky Marciano wins the **World Heavyweight Championship** title which he holds until 1956.

1953 Italian Alberto Ascari wins the **F1 Driver's Championship** for the second consecutive time, driving a Ferrari on both occasions.

Ken Rosewall won the **Australian Open** for his first grand slam title at just 18 years of age.

Maureen Connolly (USA) becomes the first woman to win the **Grand Slam** in tennis. The Australian Open, the French Open, Wimbledon and the US Open.

1954 At the **FIFA World Cup** held in Switzerland, Hungary squandered a 2-0 lead over West Germany to lose the final 3-2. Considered to be one of the most disappointing finals matches ever.

In **Athletics**, English runner Roger Bannister becames the first person in history to run one mile in under four minutes.

1955 In US thoroughbred **Horse Racing**, 'Nashua' beats 'Swaps' at Washington Park, 'Swaps' only loss in 9 starts. Nashua's owner-breeder, William Woodward Jr. dreams of owning a Derby winner but is shot dead by his wife before he can send 'Nashua' to England to train.

1956 Lew Hoad wins the **Australian Open** for his first grand slam title. He also wins the **French Open** and **Wimbledon** this year.

In **Cricket**, England off-spinner Jim Laker gains a world record taking 19 wickets in the Test match against Australia at Old Trafford. He takes a total of 46 wickets in the five Tests, a record in an England-Australia series.

1957 Jacques Anquetil of France wins the **Tour de France** for the first of his five times.

In **Football**, Stanley Matthews, 'The Wizard of the Dribble' and 'The Magician' makes his last appearance for England in the match against Denmark in Copenhagen.

1958 Pelé makes his debut at the **FIFA World Cup** in Sweden. Brazil defeats the host in the finals to win the cup.

The plane carrying the **Manchester United football team** crashes at Munich Airport, killing 44 people, including eight Manchester United players.

1959 Maria Bueno of Brazil won the **Wimbledon** Ladies Final at 19 years of age, her first grand slam title. She also won the **US Open** that year.

South African golfer, Gary Player, wins his first major title at **The Open** Championship.

The **Rugby** Five Nations Championship is won by France, the team's first outright championship title.

Swimming the English Channel

On 8th August 1950, Florence Chadwick, 'Queen of the Channel', set a new Women's record for swimming the 21 miles of the English Channel from France to England, in 13 hrs 20 mins.

Florence was a typist and swimming coach from California and achieved four successes in her ten attempts. In 1951 she became the first ever woman, at 32 years old, to swim from England to France, which also made her the first woman to ever swim the 'double'.

She made three England to France swims and each one took the record for the fastest time, going from 16 hrs 22 mins in 1951 to 13 hrs 55 mins in 1955. On her last three successful swims she also attempted to swim there-and-back but gave up on the return legs.

The first woman to ever swim the Channel was also an American, Gertrude Ederle, who in 1926, achieved a time of 14 hrs and 34 mins.

The first person to successfully cross the stretch of water was Captain Matthew Webb, who swam the distance in 1875 at his second attempt and took 21 hrs 45 mins.

Juan Manuel Fangio

In May 1950, the Formula One world championship era began, at Silverstone with Alfa Romeo becoming its first super-power, sweeping to victory at the start of the season and remaining unbeaten until the end. The Argentinian driver, a stocky, balding Argentine already in his 40s and nicknamed, 'El Chueco', the 'bowlegged or bandy legged one', dominated the first decade of Formula One, winning the World Driver's Championship five times. He raced for four different teams, Alfa Romeo, Ferrari, Mercedes-Benz and Maserati, winning 24 of his 52 F1 races, including his 'home' Grand Prix in Argentina four times.

At this time F1 cars were fast and physically demanding to drive, races were long and by the end of a GP, drivers often suffered blistered hands from the heavy steering and gear changing and their faces were sometimes covered in soot from the inboard brakes. In 1955, Fangio was teamed with a 25-year-old 'apprentice', Stirling Moss, Britain's brightest prospect.

TRANSPORT

By 1950, Britain was the world's biggest car exporter and most cars on our roads were built in Britain. Here are some of the famous cars.

Ford Popular

When launched in 1953, the Ford Popular was the cheapest car in Britain. But while robust and reliable, it was quite basic; even sun visors cost extra.

Vauxhall Cresta

While Vauxhall's Cresta brought a touch of chrome-clad American glamour to British roads in the 1950s these large cars often succumbed to rust. More than 300,000 were built in Luton from 1948 to 1965.

The Last Steam Trains

Great Britain was the first nation to use steam locomotives and Britain's railway is the oldest in the world but by 1955, a modernisation programme started to replace this vital cog of the nineteenth century industrial revolution with diesel and electric trains.

Morris Minor

More than 1.6 million of this design classic were manufactured and the Minor Series II and Minor 1000 belong to the 1950s.

The Mini

The Mini may be the greatest British classic car of all time. In 1959, Sir Alec Issigonis created a vehicle where passengers used 80% of its interior space. The Mini became an iconic, affordable, family car.

Jaguar XK140

A beautiful sports car with a sleek bonnet and sparkling wheels

Britain's First Motorway

In December 1958, Prime Minister Harold Macmillan opened the Preston Bypass, the first ever section of motorway in Great Britain, planned as part of a larger scheme to build a north-south motorway network.

Nearly £3 million was spent on the construction of this original 8 ¼ mile, dual two lane, motorway after early work was hampered by foul weather and heavy rainfall which resulted in the postponement of various heavy engineering works. Ultimately, this meant the initial two-year plan was delayed by a further five months.

The following year, the first section of the M1 motorway was opened in November 1959 and with it, the first service station at Watford Gap. Initially there was no speed limit on the motorway and, over three lanes, it gave motorists the chance to drive 50 miles from St Albans to Rugby as fast as their car could manage. The design team anticipated that the road would cope with about 14,000 vehicles each day.

The De Havilland Comet

On 2nd May 1952, the Comet 1 airliner carried passengers on a scheduled commercial route for the very first time. The journey from London to Johannesburg was reportedly a sublimely smooth one. This new aircraft could carry 36 passengers, those in first class sat around tables, at a cruising speed of 450 mph – and a top speed of 503 mph - over a distance of 2,500 miles and BOAC's fleet was the envy of world airlines.

Despite the aim to provide affordable widespread travel in an age where air travel was still the preserve of the rich, the Comet attracted its fair share of highly esteemed passengers. Queen Elizabeth, Princess Margaret and the Queen Mother were all guests of Sir Geoffrey and Lady de Havilland on a special flight in June 1953 and became the first members of the Royal Family to fly by jet.

The advent of passenger jets transformed air travel. Between 1950 and 1960 the number of air passengers carried in the UK increased from just over one million to six million.

1960

May: Princess Margaret marries photographer, Anthony Armstrong-Jones at Westminster Abbey. It is the first royal marriage to be televised.

Nov: "Lady Chatterley's Lover" sells 200,000 copies in one day following its publication since the ban enforced in 1928 is lifted.

1961

Jan: The farthing, used since the 13th Century, ceases to be legal tender in the UK.

Apr: The US attack on "The Bay of Pigs" in Cuba was defeated within two days by Cuban forces under the direct command of their Premier, Fidel Castro.

1962

Jan: An outbreak of smallpox infects 45 and kills 19 in South Wales. 900,000 people in the region are vaccinated against the disease.

Dec: The "Big Freeze" starts in Britain. There are no frost-free nights until 5 March 1963.

1963

June: Kennedy: 'Ich bin ein Berliner' The US President Kennedy, has made a ground-breaking speech in Berlin offering American solidarity to the citizens of West Germany.

Aug: 'The Great Train Robbery' on the travelling Post Office train from Glasgow to Euston, takes place in Buckinghamshire.

1964

Mar: Radio Caroline, the 'pirate radio station' begins regular broadcasting from a ship just outside UK territorial waters off Felixstowe, Suffolk.

Oct: After thirteen years in power, the Conservatives are beaten by Labour at the General Election and Harold Wilson becomes Prime Minister.

The Tiller Girls At The London Palladium

1962: In April, the five-month-old strike by Equity, the actors' union, against the Independent television companies, ends, with actors gaining huge increases in basic pay rates.

1963: John F. Kennedy, the 35th president of the United States, was assassinated on November 22 in Dallas, Texas, while riding in a presidential motorcade. He was with his wife Jacqueline, Texas Governor John Connally, and Connally's wife Nellie when he was fatally shot from a nearby building by Lee Harvey Oswald. Governor Connally was seriously wounded in the attack. The motorcade rushed to the local hospital, where Kennedy was pronounced dead about 30 minutes after the shooting. Mr Connally recovered.

1969 APOLLO 11. Neil Armstrong becomes the first man to walk on the moon. "One small step for man, one giant leap for mankind."

1965: In January, Sir Winston Churchill dies aged 90. Sir Winston served as Prime Minister of the United Kingdom from 1940-45 and again from 1951-1955. He is best known for his wartime leadership as PM.

1965

Mar: 3,500 US Marines, the first American ground combat troops arrive in Da Nang, South Vietnam.

Aug: Elizabeth Lane is appointed as the first ever female High Court Judge. She is assigned to the Family Division.

1966

Jun: The first British credit card, the Barclaycard, is introduced by Barclays. It has a monopoly in the market until the Access Card is introduced in 1972.

Sept: HMS Resolution is launched at Barrow-in-Furness. It is the first of the Polaris ballistic missile submarines, armed with 16 Polaris A missiles.

1967

Jan: Donald Campbell, the racing driver and speedboat racer, was killed on Coniston Water whilst attempting to break his own speed record.

Dec: The Anglo-French Concorde supersonic aircraft was unveiled in Toulouse, France.

1968

Jun: The National Health Service reintroduces prescription charges, abolished by the Labour Govt. in 1965, at 2s 6d.

Sep: The General Post Office divides their single rate postal service into two. First-class letters at 5d and second-class at 4d.

1969

Mar: The Queen opens the Victoria Line on the London Underground. It is the first entirely new Underground line in London for 50 years.

Dec: The abolition of the death penalty for murder, having been suspended since 1965, was made permanent by Parliament.

At the beginning of the decade, the wireless was still the usual form of entertainment in the home and children could sit comfortably to "Listen with Mother" on the Light Programme and mother could carry on listening to "Woman's Hour" afterwards.

However, television was becoming increasingly affordable, and the two channels, BBC and ITV were joined in 1965 by BBC2. Dr Finlay's Casebook; The Black and White Minstrel Show; Top of the Pops; Perry Mason and Z Cars were the most popular shows of the 60's.

In 1962 the BBC bravely introduced a new satirical show, "That Was the Week That Was" which proved a big hit and by 1969, the BBC was converting programmes to colour.

Children's pocket money, probably 6d (2.5p) a week in the early years, could buy sweets. Black Jacks and Fruit Salads (4 for a penny (0.5p)), sweet cigarettes, lemonade crystals, gob stoppers, flying saucers or toffees, weighed by the shopkeeper in 2oz or 4oz paper bags. All could be eaten whilst reading a copy of The Beano or Dandy, Bunty or Jack and Jill comics.

The simple, yet addictive party game Twister was introduced in 1966.

In the 60's the nuclear family was still the norm, father out at work and mother busy with the housework which was time consuming before the general possession of electrical labour-saving devices.

Washing up was done by hand and laundry gradually moved to machines over the decade.

Twin tubs, one for washing and one for Spinning, became popular in the late 60's and were usually wheeled into the kitchen to be attached to the cold tap and afterwards, have the waste-water emptied into the sink. The 'housewife' had to be at home to transfer the wet washing from the washing tub to the spinning tub.

By the end of the 60's, 58% of households had a small refrigerator but no fridge/freezers, so shopping was still done regularly and, typically, meals were home cooked.

Chicken was expensive but beef was cheaper and olive oil came only in tiny bottles from the chemist to help clean your ears!

In Britain, the domestic freezer is still a luxury but by the mid 60's, some 700m fish fingers were among the 60,000 tons of frozen fish consumed with peas from 35,000 acres and 120,000 quick-frozen chickens.

Goods came to you. The milkman delivered the milk to your doorstep, the baker brought the baskets of bread to the door, the greengrocer delivered and the 'pop man' came once a week with 'dandelion and burdock', 'cherryade' or 'cream soda' and the rag and bone man called down the street for your recycling.

ART AND CULTURE

1960 - 1963

1960   Frederick Ashton's 'La Fille Mal Gardée' premieres by The Royal Ballet at the Royal Opera House.

In court, Penguin Books who published 'Lady Chatterley's Lover' by DH Lawrence, is found not guilty of obscenity.

1961   The 'Betting & Gaming Act' comes into force which allows the operating of commercial Bingo halls.

'Ken' is introduced in the US as a boyfriend for 'Barbie'.

1962   Margot Fonteyn and Rudolf Nureyev first dance together in a Royal Ballet performance of Giselle, in London.

Dec John Steinbeck, American author is awarded the Nobel Prize in Literature. Aleksandr Solzhenitsyn's novella, "One Day in the Life of Ivan Denisovich" is published in Russia.

1963   The first Leeds Piano Competition is held, and Michael Roll is the winner.

Authors CS Lewis and Aldous Huxley both die on 23 November, but news of their deaths is overshadowed by the assassination of JFK.

Margot Fonteyn and Robert Helpmann performing The Sleeping Beauty.

Their partnership has been described as the greatest of all time.

1964 - 1969

1964   BBC television airs the first 'Top of the Pops'. Dusty Springfield is the very first artist to perform, with 'I Only Want to Be With You'.

Ernest Hemingway's memoirs of his years in Paris, 'A Moveable Feast' is published posthumously by his wife.

1965   Rembrandt's painting 'Titus' is sold at Christie's London fetching the then record price of 760,000 guineas. (£798,000).

The f*** word is spoken for the first time on television by Kenneth Tynan and two weeks later, Mary Whitehouse founds The National Viewers' and Listeners' Association.

1966   'Rosencrantz and Guildenstern Are Dead' by Tom Stoppard has its debut at the Edinburgh Festival Fringe.

BBC1 televises 'Cathy Come Home', a docudrama that is viewed by a quarter of the British public and goes on to influence attitudes to homelessness.

1967   **'The Summer of Love'.** Thousands of young 'flower children' descend on the west coast of America, for hippie music, hallucinogenic drugs, spiritual meditation and free-love.

BBC radio restructures. The Home Service becomes Radio 4, the Third Programme becomes Radio 3 and the Light Programme is split between Radio 1 (to compete with pirate radio) and Radio 2.

1968   The BBC repeat of the twenty-six episodes of 'The Forsyte Saga' on Sunday evening television, leads to reports of 'publicans and vicars complaining it was driving away their customers and worshippers, respectively' and of 'Evensong services being moved to avoid a clash'.

1969   The Beatles perform together for the last time on the rooftop of Apple Records in London. The impromptu concert was broken up by the police.

The three-day Woodstock Music Festival was held in August 1969 on a dairy farm in Bethel, New York. Nearly half a million young people arrived for "An Aquarian Experience: 3 Days of Peace and Music." Now known simply as Woodstock, the festival was a huge success, but it did not go off without a hitch. The almost 500,000 people who turned up was unexpected and caused the organisers a headache which necessitated venue changes and this was before the bad weather, muddy conditions, lack of food and unsanitary conditions made life even more difficult.

Surprisingly, the event passed off peacefully, this fact attributed by most, to the amount of sex, psychedelic drugs and rock 'n roll that took place. Others say, couples were too busy 'making love not war' to cause trouble, either way, Woodstock earned its place in the halls of pop culture history fame.

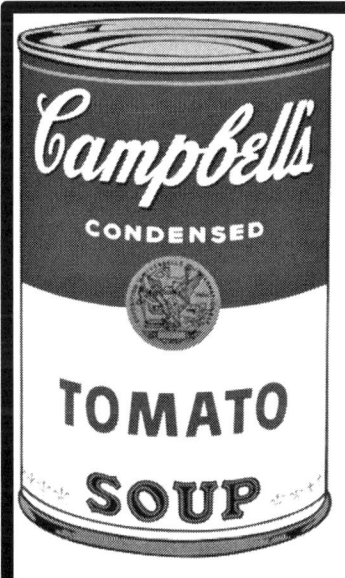

"American artist Andy Warhol premieres his "Campbell's Soup Cans" exhibit in Los Angeles".

Andy Warhol famously borrowed familiar icons from everyday life and the media, among them celebrity and tabloid news photos, comic strips, and, in this work, the popular canned soup made by the Campbell's Soup Company. When he first exhibited "Campbell's Soup Cans", the images were displayed together on shelves, like products in a grocery aisle. At the time, Campbell's sold 32 soup varieties and each one of Warhol's 32 canvases corresponds to a different flavour, each having a different label. The first flavour, introduced in 1897, was tomato.

Each canvas was hand painted and the fleur de lys pattern round each can's bottom edge was hand stamped. Warhol said, "I used to drink Campbell's Soup. I used to have the same lunch every day, for 20 years, I guess!"

FILMS

1960 - 1963

1960   **Ben Hur**, the religious epic, was a remake of a 1925 silent film with a similar title and had the largest budget ($15.175m) and the largest sets built of any film produced at the time.

1961   Billy Wilder's risqué tragi-comedy **The Apartment** won the Academy Award for Best Picture. Starring Jack Lemmon and Shirley MacLaine, it tells a story of an ambitious, lonely insurance clerk who lends out his New York apartment to executives for their love affairs.

1962   New Films released this year included, **Lolita** starring James Mason and Sue Lyon. **Dr No**, the first James Bond film, starring Sean Connery and Ursula Andress and **What Ever Happened to Baby Jane?** a horror film with Bette Davis

1963   **Lawrence of Arabia,** based on author TS Eliot's book 'Seven Pillars of Wisdom' and starring Peter O'Toole and Alec Guinness won the Oscar for Best Picture.
The publicity of the affair between the stars, Elizabeth Taylor and Richard Burton, helped make **Cleopatra** a huge box office success but the enormous production costs, caused the film to be a financial disaster.

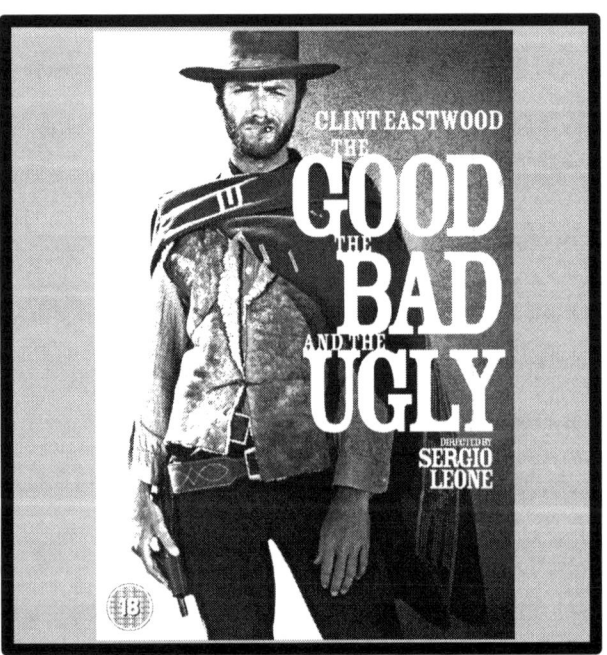

1964 - 1969

1964   The historical adventure, sex comedy romp **Tom Jones** won four Oscars, Best Picture, Best Director, Best Adapted Screenplay and Best Musical Score. Albert Finney starred as the titular hero and Susannah York as the girl he loves.

1965   Winning the Oscar this year, the film **My Fair Lady,** based on George Bernard Shaw's play 'Pygmalion', tells the story of Eliza Doolittle and her quest to 'speak proper' in order to be presentable in Edwardian London's high society. Rex Harrison and Audrey Hepburn starred and it became the 2nd highest grossing film of the year just behind **The Sound of Music** which won the Academy Award the following year.

1966   **The Good, the Bad and the Ugly** was directed by Sergio Leonie, the Italian director who gave rise to the term 'spaghetti western'- a genre of westerns produced and directed by Italians. Clint Eastwood was the Good, Lee Van Cleef, the Bad and Eli Wallach, the Ugly. The film was a huge success and catapulted Clint Eastwood to fame.

1967   The fun filled seduction of Benjamin Braddock by Mrs Robinson in **The Graduate** made the film the biggest grossing production of the year world-wide.

1968   The famous quote "They call me Mister Tibbs" comes from **In the Heat of the Night** where Sidney Poitier plays Virgil Tibbs, a black police detective from Philadelphia, caught up in a murder investigation in racially hostile Mississippi. Rod Steiger is the white chief of police.

1969   **Oliver** the musical based on Dicken's novel and Lionel Bart's stage show, carried off the Oscar for Best Picture.

Editor's Note: The Academy Awards are held in February and each year's awards are presented for films that were first shown during the full preceding calendar year from January 1 to December 31 Los Angelis, California. Source: Wikipedia

HARRY SALTZMAN and **ALBERT R. BROCCOLI** PRESENT

THE FIRST JAMES BOND FILM!

IAN FLEMING'S

DR. NO

TECHNICOLOR

SEAN CONNERY AS 007

ANDRESS · WISEMAN · LOI

MAIBAUM HARWOOD MATHER YOUNG SALT.

This was the first-ever launch of a James Bond film in a cinema and was attended by the stars, Sean Connery and Ursula Andress together with the James Bond creator Ian Fleming. The plot of this British spy film revolves around James Bond who needs to solve the mystery of the strange disappearance of a British agent to Jamaica and finds an underground base belonging to Dr No who is plotting to disrupt the American space launch with a radio beam weapon. The film was condemned by The Vatican as "a dangerous mixture of violence, vulgarity, sadism, and sex".

1962 : "West Side Story" Wins The Academy Awards "Best Picture" category.

The musical with lyrics by Stephen Sondheim and music by Leonard Bernstein was inspired by the story of William Shakespeare's "Romeo and Juliet". Set in the mid 1950s in Upper West Side of New York City, which was then, a cosmopolitan working-class area, it follows the rivalry between the Jets and the Sharks, two teenage street gangs from different ethnic backgrounds.

The Sharks are from Puerto Rico and are taunted by the white Jets gang. The hero, Tony, a former member of the Jets falls in love with Maria, the sister of the leader of the Sharks. The sophisticated music and the extended dance scenes, focussing on the social problems marked a turning point in musical theatre. The film starred Natalie Wood and Richard Beymer.

73

FASHION

CHANGING FASHION

It was a decade of three parts for fashion. The first years were reminiscent of the fifties, conservative and restrained, classic in style and design. Jackie Kennedy, the President's glamorous wife, was very influential with her tailored suit dresses and pill box hats, white pearls and kitten heels.

The hairdresser was of extreme importance. Beehive coiffures worn by the likes of Dusty Springfield and Brigitte Bardot were imitated by women of all ages and Audrey Hepburn popularised the high bosom, sleeveless dress. Whilst low, square toed shoes were high fashion, 'on the street', stilettos rivalled them.

THE MODS

In the mid-60s, the look had become sleeker and more modern. The lines were form-fitting but didn't try to accentuate curves. There were brighter colours and for the young, the Mod style.

Male mods took on a smooth, sophisticated look that included tailor-made suits with narrow lapels, thin ties, button-down collar shirts and wool jumpers.

The pea coat and Chelsea boots looked very 'London'. The Beatles were leading the way, hair started to grow longer, and trousers lost the baggy, comfortable fit of the 1950's.

For girls, shift dresses and mini skirts became shorter and shorter, worn with flat shoes or 'go go boots', short hair with eyebrow brushing fringes, and little makeup, just a pale lipstick and false eyelashes.

Slender models like Jean Shrimpton and Twiggy exemplified the look and new, exciting designers emerged such as Mary Quant. Television shows like 'Ready Steady Go!' showed their audiences at home, what they should be wearing.

IN THE 1960S

THE HIPPIES

For the young, jeans were becoming ubiquitous both for men and women, skin-tight drainpipes through to the flared bottoms of the late years. London had taken over from Paris to become the fashion centre of the world and in contrast to the beginning of the decade, the end was the exact opposite.

Bright, swirling colours. Psychedelic, tie-dye shirts, long hair and beards were commonplace. Individualism was the word and mini skirts were worn alongside brightly coloured and patterned tunics with flowing long skirts.

CARNABY STREET

By 1967, Carnaby Street was popular with followers of the mod and hippie styles. Many fashion designers, such as Mary Quant, Lord John and Irvine Sellars, had premises there, and underground music bars, such as the Roaring Twenties, opened in the surrounding streets.

Bands such as the Small Faces, The Who and The Rolling Stones appeared in the area, to work at the legendary Marquee Club round the corner in Wardour Street, to shop, and to socialise. The Street became one of the coolest destinations associated with 1960s Swinging London.

LEISURE

THE PACKAGE HOLIDAY

By the mid-sixties, the traditional British seaside holiday, sandcastles, donkey rides, sticks of rock and fish and chips on the beach was gradually giving way to the new and exciting Package Holiday in the sun.

Tour operators began taking plane loads of holidaymakers abroad, almost exclusively to Europe and to Spain in particular. Hotels were springing up everywhere, often obscuring the 'exotic views' that the tourists were promised and were basic with rather simple local fare, which even then was not to the taste of a large majority. Restaurants flourished with 'Full English Breakfast' posters displayed all over the windows, tea and beer were in demand.

By the end of the decade, Luton Airport, a favourite with the tour firms, had flights arriving back every hour full of sunburnt Brits wearing sombreros and clutching Spanish donkeys and maracas.

A cold British beach holiday was replaced for many by cheap package holidays to sunny Spain.

"LET'S GO FOR A CHINESE"

A 'Greasy Spoon'

A cheese-pineapple hedgehog

In the early 1960s, eating out was expensive and apart from 'greasy spoon' cafes, or a packet of salted crisps at a pub, dining out was limited to formal restaurants. However, with a rise in immigrants from Asia, Chinese and Indian restaurants were springing up and their relatively affordable and tasty food became so popular that Vesta brought out their first 'foreign convenience' foods, the Vesta Curries and Vesta Chow Mein.

A cheaper alternative was inviting friends to eat at home, and the dinner party boomed from the end of the decade. Pre-dinner drinks were often served with cubes of tinned pineapple and cheddar cheese on sticks, stuck into half a tinfoil covered grapefruit to look like a hedgehog – the height of 60s sophistication! The main course might feature the fashionable 'spaghetti bolognese', and 'Blue Nun', Mateus Rosé or Chianti wine, adding a hint of sophistication to the new 'smart' set's evening.

IN THE 1960s

Teenage Leisure

The 60's became the era for the teenager, but it started off with the same disciplines as the fifties. At school the teachers commanded respect and gave out punishment when it was not given. Parents could determine when and where their children could be out of house, gave sons and daughters chores to do and families ate together and watched television together.

Scouts and Guides were still very popular and a natural progression from the years as Cubs and Brownies and Outward Bounding or working for the Duke of Edinburgh Awards remained popular for many, but as the decade wore on, the lure of the new found freedom for the young was hard for many to overcome. Coffee bars became the place to meet, drink coffee or chocolate, listen to the latest hits on the juke box and talk with friends. The political climate influenced them, they demonstrated in the streets against the Vietnam War, for civil rights and to 'Ban the Bomb'. They developed the 'hippie' point of view, advocating non-violence and love, and by the end of the decade, "Make Love not War" was the 'flower children's' mantra.

Outdoor music festivals sprang up all over the country and thousands of, usually mud-caked, teenagers gathered to listen to their favourite artists, rock concerts played to packed houses and the young experimented with marijuana and LSD. Psychedelic art was incorporated into films, epitomised by the Beatles' 'Yellow Submarine'.

1960   Poor Me by Adam Faith, a teen idol, reached number 1 and stayed there for two weeks whilst his previous number 1 hit, **What Do You Want** was still in the top ten. The Everly Brothers, the American rock duo, had their fifth number 1 with **Cathy's Clown**. Their first was Bye Bye Love in 1957. A surprise number 1 for four weeks was by Lonnie Donnegan, the skiffle singer, with **My Old Man's a Dustman.**

1961   Wooden Heart sung by Elvis Presley stayed at number 1 for six weeks and became the best-selling UK single of the year. Johnny Leyton had a three-week number 1 with **Johnny Remember Me** in August and it returned to the number 1 spot again at the end of September. Teenage singer and actress Helen Shapiro, had her second number one, **Walkin' Back to Happiness**, whilst still only fifteen.

1962   The top selling single of the year was by the Australian singer, Frank Ifield. **I Remember You** was sung in a yodelling, country-music style.
Acker Bilk's **Stranger on the Shore** becomes the first British recording to reach the number 1 spot on the US Billboard Hot 100.
The Rolling Stones make their debut at London's Marquee Club, opening for Long John Baldry.

1962: The Rolling Stones make their debut at London's Marquee Club playing the rock n' roll of Chuck Berry and Bo Diddley.

1963   The Beatles have three number 1's in the UK charts in their first year. **From Me to You, She Loves You** and **I Want to Hold Your Hand.** Their debut album, **Please Please Me**, reaches the top of the album charts.
Produced by Phil Spector, The Crystals have a hit with **And Then He Kissed Me**
How Do You Do What You Do to Me, the debut single by Liverpudlian band Gerry and the Pacemakers, stays at number 1 for three weeks in April.

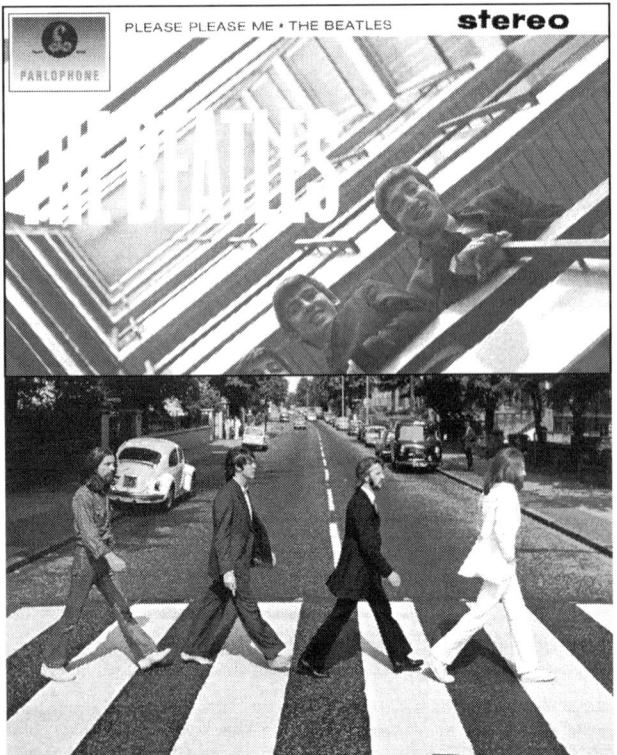

1964 The Hollies, the Merseybeat group founded by school friends Allan Clarke and Graham Nash, reach number 2 in the UK charts with **Just One Look**, a cover of the song by Doris Troy in the US.
Originally written by Burt Bacharach for Dionne Warwick, **Anyone Who Had a** Heart, sung by Cilla Black, became a UK number 1 for three weeks and was also the fourth best-selling single of 1964 in the UK, with sales of around 950,000 copies.

"The Fab Four", John Lennon, Paul McCartney, George Harrison and Ringo Star were the ultimate pop phenomenon of the '60s.

1965 Unchained Melody by The Righteous Brothers, with a solo by Bobby Hatfield becomes a jukebox standard. **Its Not Unusual** sung by Tom Jones becomes an international hit after being promoted by the offshore, pirate radio station, Radio Caroline. **Get Off of My Cloud** by The Rolling Stones was written by Mick Jagger and Keith Richards as a single to follow their previous hit of the year, **(I Can't Get No) Satisfaction**.

1966 Nancy Sinatra with **These Boots Are Made for Walkin'** reaches number 1.
Good Vibrations sung by The Beach Boys, becomes an immediate hit both sides of the Atlantic.
Ike and Tina Turner released **River Deep, Mountain High** and their popularity soars in the UK after a tour with The Rolling Stones.

1967 Waterloo Sunset by The Kinks, written by Ray Davies, reached number 2 in the British charts and was a top 10 hit in Australia, New Zealand and most of Europe. In North America, it failed to chart.
A Whiter Shade of Pale the debut single by Procul Harem stays at number 1 for eight weeks.
Sandie Shaw wins the Eurovision Song Contest with **Puppet on a String**.

1968 Dusty Springfield's **Son of a Preacher Man** was her last top thirty hit until her collaboration with The Pet Shop Boys in 1987. In 1994, **Preacher Man** was included in Tarantino's film 'Pulp Fiction'.
Manfred Mann has a resounding success with **Mighty Quinn**, their third UK number 1 and third hit singing a song written by Bob Dylan.
The comedy group The Scaffold's record, **Lily the Pink** released in November became number 1 for the four weeks over the Christmas holidays.

1969 **Where Do You Go To (My Lovely)?** by the British singer-songwriter Peter Sarstedt stayed at number 1 for four weeks.
I Heard It Through the Grapevine was written in 1966 and recorded by Gladys Knight and the Pips. However, it was the version by Marvin Gaye that took the number 1 spot in the UK for three weeks and became the biggest hit single on the Motown label.
Je t'aime… moi non plus was written in 1967 for Brigitte Bardot but Serge Gainsbourg and Jane Birkin recorded the best known version and the duet reached number 1 in the UK. It was banned in several countries due to its overtly sexual content.

SCIENCE AND NATURE

THE LONDON SMOG

Britain still experienced "pea-soupers" in the 60's and in December 1962, London suffered under a choking blanket of smog. After three days, the noxious layer spread all over the country.

Smog is a concentration of smoke particles and other substances such as sulphur dioxide, combined with fog in conditions of low temperature, high pressure and lack of wind. Visibility was reduced such that a light could only be seen at 50ft and in spite of people covering their faces with scarves, surgical masks or handkerchiefs, the overwhelming smell of sulphur and coal smoke left an unpleasant metallic taste in the mouth and irritated eyes and noses. Bronchitis increased significantly and it is estimated that, in Greater London alone, there were 700 deaths in total.

In 1962, the Duke of Edinburgh was in New York for the inaugural dinner of the US branch of the World Wildlife Fund, first set up in Zurich in 1961, and warned his audience that our descendants could be forced to live in a world where the only living creature would be man himself -"*always assuming,*" he said, "*that we don't destroy ourselves as well in the meantime.*"

In his speech, the Duke described poachers who were threatening extermination of many big game animals in Africa as "killers for profit … the get-rich-at-any-price mob." African poachers, he said, were killing off the rhinoceros to get its horn for export to China, "*where, for some incomprehensible reason, they seem to think it acts as an aphrodisiac.*" The Duke also criticised the status seekers – people "like the eagle chasers". The bald eagle in North America was being chased and killed by people in light aeroplanes who seem to think it smart to own its feathers and claws.

"*What is needed, above all now,*" he said, "*are people all over the world who understand the problem and really care about it. People who have the courage to see that the conservation laws are obeyed.*"

DUKE OF EDINBURGH LAUNCHES WORLD WILDLIFE FUND

IN THE 1960s

Write-Protect Tab Supply Reel Slip Sheet Take-up Reel

Guide Roller Magnetic Shield Pressure Pad Capstan Hole

THE CASSETTE TAPE

The cassette tape was first developed by Philips in Belgium in 1962. These two small spools inside its plastic case, which wind magnetic-coated film on which the audio content is stored and pass it from one side to the other, meant music could now be recorded and shared by everyone.

Up until now, music was typically recorded on vinyl which needed a record player, or on reel-to-reel recorders which were comparatively expensive and difficult to use and neither of which were portable. The cassette player allowed individuals to record their favourite songs easily and also take their music with them "on-the-go". Music lovers soon learned how to create their own mixed tapes, for themselves or to share with friends.

More than 3 billion tapes were sold between 1962 and 1988.

THE ABERFAN DISASTER

On 21 October 1966, the worst mining-related disaster in British history took place in Aberfan, in South Wales. Coal was mined there for domestic heating and the waste was dumped at the top of the valley on land of no economic value. But crucially, it was tipped on highly porous sandstone which overlaid at least one natural spring.

During October 1966 heavy rainfall led to a build-up of water within this tip and caused it to collapse. With a deafening roar, 107 cu m of black slurry turned into an avalanche. The deluge leapt over the old railway embankment into the village where destroyed 18 houses and Pant Glas Junior School together with part of the neighbouring County Secondary School.

In total, 144 lives were lost, 116 of them children, 109 of these were aged between seven and ten and died in their classrooms on the last day before half term. Of the 28 adults who died, five were primary school teachers.

The official inquiry placed the blame entirely on the National Coal Board.

1960 - 1969

1960   In tennis, Rod Laver wins his first grand slam title as a 21-year-old taking the **Australian Open.**
Jack Brabham wins the **F1 driver's championship** for the second straight time.

1961   Five Nations Championship (now 6 Nations) rugby series is won by France.
Tottenham Hotspur beat Leicester City 2-0 in the **FA Cup Final**.

1962   Sonny Liston knocks out Floyd Pattison after two minutes into the first round of the "Boxing World Title" fight in Chicago.

1963   Mill House, at 18 hands, known as 'The Big Horse', wins the **Cheltenham Gold Cup.**

1964   The **Tour de France i**s won by Jacques Anquetil of France, the first cyclist to win the Tour five times. 1957 and 1961-64.

1965   At the **Masters** in Atlanta, Jack Nicklaus shoots a record 17 under par to win the tournament.
In the **FA Cup Final** at Wembley, Liverpool beats Leeds United 2-1.

1966   England defeat Germany to win the **FIFA World Cup**

1967   Defending champion Billie Jean King defeats Ann Haydon-Jones in the **Wimbledon Women's Singles Championship**.
The New York Yacht Club retains the **America's Cup** when 'Intrepid' beat the Australian challenger 'Dame Pattie', 4 races to 1.

1968   English International cricketer Basil D'Oliveira, of 'Cape Coloured' background, is excluded from the **MCC South African tour** side, leading to turmoil in the world of cricket.

1969   The Grand National is won by 12-year-old Highland Wedding by 12 lengths.

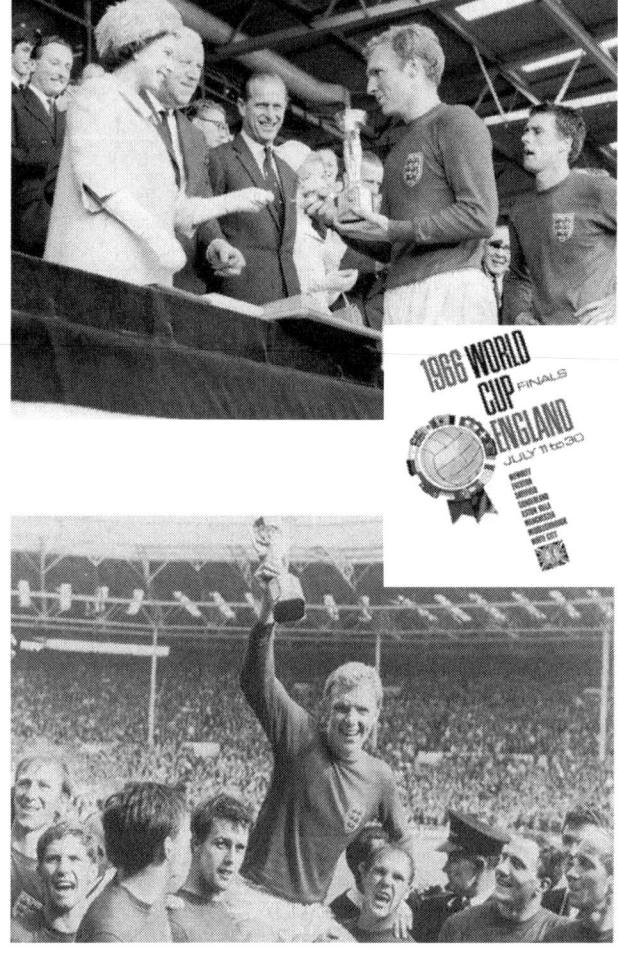

1966 FIFA WORLD CUP

On July 30th, England and West Germany lined up at Wembley to determine the winner of the 'Jules Rimet Trophy', the prize for winning the World Cup. England won 4-2 after extra time and the match is remembered for Geoff Hurst's hat-trick and the controversial third goal awarded to England by the referee and linesman.

In addition to an attendance of 96,924 at the stadium, the British television audience peaked at 32.3 million viewers, making it the UK's most-watched television event ever.

It was the first occasion that England had hosted, or won, the World Cup and was to remain their only major tournament win. It was also the nation's last final at a major international football tournament for 55 years, until 2021 when England reached the Euro Final but lost to Italy after a penalty shootout.

1964 OLYMPIC GAMES

In 1964, the first Olympic Games to be held in Asia, took place in Japan during October to avoid the city's midsummer heat and humidity and the September typhoon season. It marked many milestones in the history of the modern Games; a cinder running track was used for the last time in the athletics events, whilst a fibreglass pole was used for the first time in the pole-vaulting competition. These Games were also the last occasion that hand timing by stopwatch was used for official timing.

25 world records were broken and 52 of a possible 61 Olympic records were also broken. Ethiopian runner Abebe Bikila won his second consecutive Olympic marathon. Bob Hayes won the men's 100 metres and then anchored the US 400 metre relay team to a world record victory. Peter Snell, the New Zealand middle-distance runner, won both the 800 and 1500 metres, the only man to have done so in the same Olympics since 1920. Ann Packer of Britain made a record-breaking debut winning gold in the 800 metres and silver in the 400 metres.

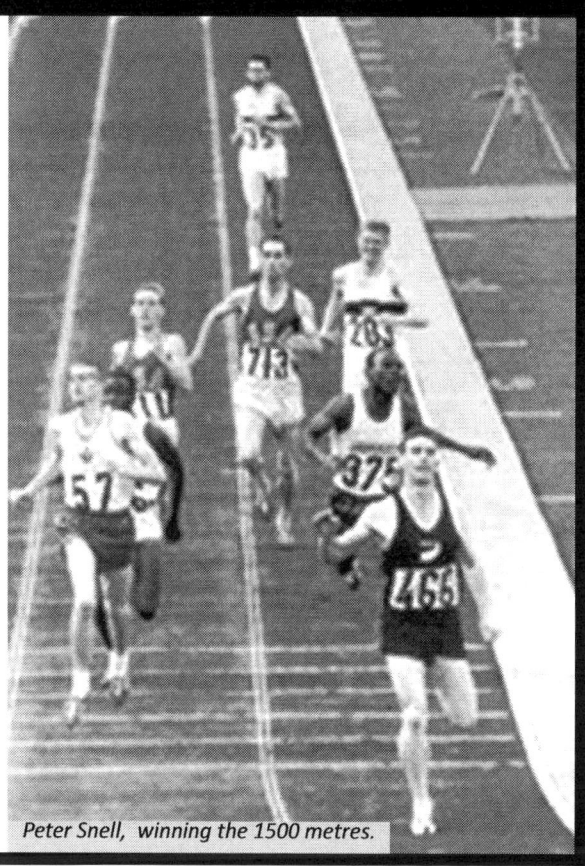

Peter Snell, winning the 1500 metres.

CASSIUS CLAY HEAVYWEIGHT CHAMPION OF THE WORLD

In 1964, Cassius Clay, later this year to be known as Muhammad Ali, fought and gained Sonny Liston's title of Heavyweight Champion of the World. The big fight took place in Miami Beach in February.

Liston was an intimidating fighter and Clay was the 7-1 under-dog, but still he engaged in taunting his opponent during the build-up to the fight, dubbing him "*the big ugly bear*", stating "*Liston even smells like a bear*" and claiming, "*After I beat him, I'm going to donate him to the zoo!*"

The result of the fight was a major upset as Clay's speed and mobility kept him out of trouble and in the third round hit Liston with a combination that opened a cut under his left eye and eventually, Liston could not come out for the seventh round.

A triumphant Clay rushed to the edge of the ring and, pointing to the ringside press, shouted: "*Eat your words!*" adding the words he was to live up to for the rest of his life, "*I am the greatest!*"

TRANSPORT

Trolleybuses were taken out of service in London in May having served since 1931.

How luxurious can an Austin Seven get?

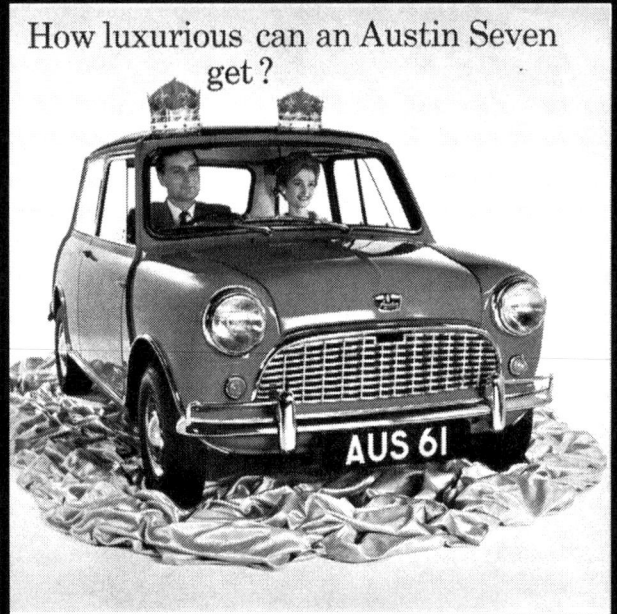

The revolutionary Mini was the fastest selling small car in Britain in the 60s. Despite the promise of the adverts early models were slow and unreliable and although promoted as a luxury family car, it was uncomfortable and cramped.

THE VICKERS VC10

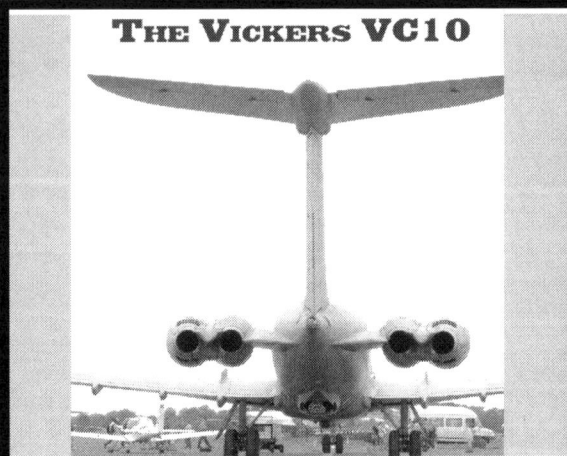

The 60's produced Britain's biggest airliner to date, the four jet Vickers VC10. With a towering tailplane, high as a four-storey house, the airliner weighed 150 tons fully loaded and was 158ft long. In service with BOAC and other airlines from the end of 1963 until 1981, the plane could carry 150 passengers at flew at 600mph over distances exceeding 4,000 miles. From 1965 they were also used as strategic air transports for the RAF.

CARS OF THE DECADE

The importance of personal transport increased dramatically during the Sixties and three of the images inextricably linked with the decade are the three-wheeler 'bubble car', the sleek, sexy, elongated E-type Jaguar and VW Camper Van.

MODS AND ROCKERS
SCOOTERS V MOTOR BIKES

Mods and Rockers were two rival British youth sub-cultures of the 1960's with a tendency to riot on Brighton beach.

They had very different outlooks: The Mods thought of themselves as sophisticated, stylish and in touch with the times. The motor cycling centred Rockers thought the Mods effeminate snobs!

They had very different appearances: Mods centred on fashion and wore suits or other clean-cut outfits. The Rockers wore black leather jackets and motorcycle boots or sometimes, 'brothel creeper' shoes.

They had very different tastes in music. The Mods favoured Soul and African American R&B. The Rockers went for Rock 'n Roll.

So not surprisingly, they had very different tastes in transport.

THE HOVERCRAFT

The great British invention of the decade was the Hovercraft. It was developed by Briton, Sir Christopher Cockerell. Saunders Roe, the flying boat firm at Cowes on the Isle of Wight built the prototype SR.N1, 20ft craft which first took to the seas in July 1959, crossing the English Channel from Calais to Dover in two hours with the inventor onboard. In 1961 hovercraft skirts were introduced to the design which provided far greater performance abilities and sea keeping.

The Hovercraft was a revolution in sea travel and the 1960's saw a fleet of craft crossing from the south coast to the Isle of Wight. They are now used throughout the world as specialised transports in disaster relief, coastguard, military and survey applications, as well as for sport or passenger service.

1970 - 1974

1970:

Jan: The age of majority for most legal purposes was reduced from 21 to 18 under terms of the Family Law Reform Act 1969.

Mar: Ian Smith declares Rhodesia a Republic and the British government refuses to recognise the new state.

1971:

Feb: Decimal Day. The UK and the Republic of Ireland both change to decimal currency.

Mar: The 'Daily Sketch', Britain's oldest tabloid newspaper is absorbed by the 'Daily Mail' after 62 years.

1972:

June: The 'Watergate' scandal begins in Richard Nixon's administration in the US.

Sep: The school leaving age in the UK was raised from 15 to 16 for pupils leaving at the end of the academic year.

1973:

Jan: The United Kingdom joins the European Economic Community, later to become the EU.

Sep: The IRA detonate bombs in Manchester and Victoria Station London and two days later, Oxford St. and Sloane Square.

1974:

Jan: Until March, the 3-day week is introduced by the Conservative Government to conserve electricity during the miners' strike.

Nov: 21 people are killed and 182 injured when the IRA set bombs in two Birmingham pubs.

1974: McDonald's open their first UK restaurant in South London. The traditional café was losing out, slow ordering and service with food served at tables was not as appealing as the clean, fast service and lower prices of this new fast food.

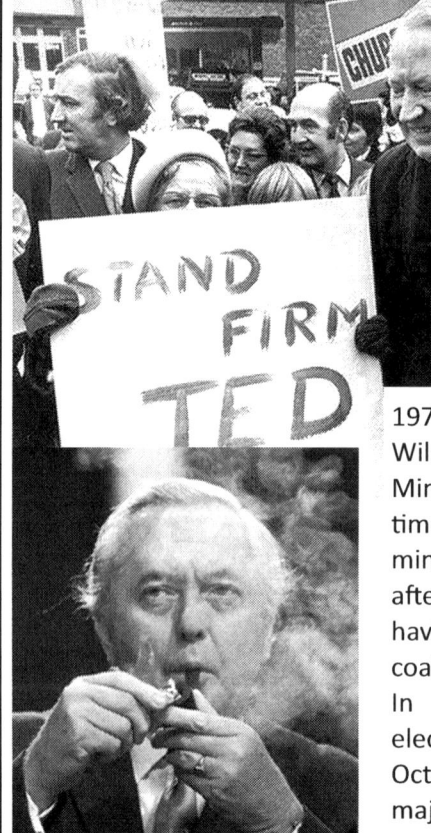

1974: In February, Harold Wilson becomes Prime Minister for the second time (first 1964-70) with a minority Government after Edward Heath resigns having failed to clinch a coalition with the Liberals. In the second general election of the year in October, Labour win with a majority of only 3 seats.

1975 - 1979

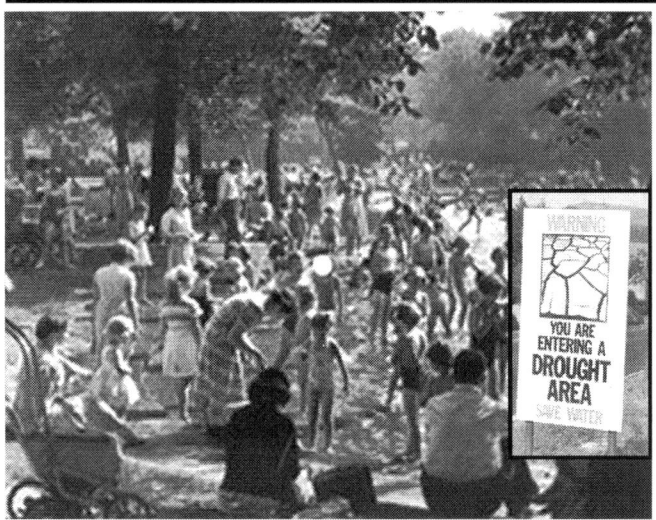

In June and July 1976, the UK experienced a heat wave. Temperatures peak at 35.9° and the whole country suffers a severe drought. Forest fires broke out, crops failed, and reservoirs dried up causing serious water shortages. The heatwave also produced swarms of ladybirds across the south and east.

On the 7th June,1977, more than one million people lined the streets of London to watch the Queen and Prince Phillip lead a procession in the golden state coach, to St Paul's at the start of a week of the Queen's Silver Jubilee celebrations – 25 years on the throne. People all over the country held street or village parties to celebrate, more than 100,000 cards were received by the Queen and 30,000 Jubilee medals were given out.

1975:
Feb: Margaret Thatcher defeats Edward Heath to become the first female leader of the Conservative Party.

Apr: The Vietnam War ends with the Fall of Saigon to the Communists. South Vietnam surrenders unconditionally.

1976:
Mar: Harold Wilson announces his resignation as Prime Minister and James Callaghan is elected to the position in April.

Oct: The Intercity 125 high speed passenger train is introduced. Initially Paddington to Bristol and south Wales.

1977:
Jan: Jimmy Carter is sworn in as the 39th President of the United States, succeeding Gerald Ford.

Sep: Freddie Laker launches his 'Skytrain' with a single fare, Gatwick to New York, at £59 compared to £189.

1978:
Aug: Louise Brown becomes the world's first human born 'in vitro fertilisation' – test tube baby.

Nov: An industrial dispute shuts down The Times newspaper – until November 1979.

1979:
Mar: Airey Neave, politician and WW2 veteran, is blown up in the House of Commons carpark by the Irish National Liberation Army.

May: Margaret Thatcher becomes the first female Prime Minister of the United Kingdom. The Conservatives win a 43 seat majority.

THE HOME

Increasing Comfort and Prosperity

Homes became brighter and more comfortable in the 1970's. Teenagers could lie on the 'impossible to clean', loopy shag pile carpet watching films on VHS video cassettes or watch live programmes on the family's colour television set.

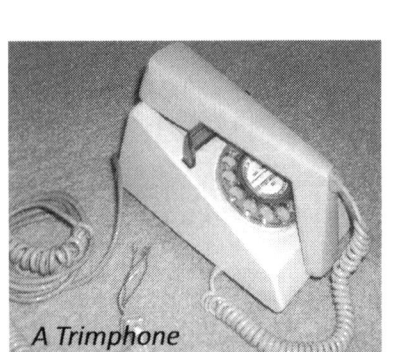

A Trimphone

The ubiquitous macramé owl, or plant holder complete with trailing spider plant, might dangle in the corner adjacent to the bulky, stone faced, rustic fireplace. Bathroom suites were often Avocado green and 'downstairs loos' were a statement of the houseowners ideals! If you were one of the 35% of households in Britain to own a telephone, you could catch up with friends and family on the new 'warbling' Trimphone, maybe sitting on your bright, floral covered couch.

Labour Saving Devices

The previous decade had been prosperous and the advances in technology continued such that by the 1970s, most households had many labour-saving devices. Sales of freezers rose rapidly in the 70s and by 1974, one in ten households had a freezer - mainly full of peas, chips and fish fingers but also ice cream, previously a rare treat, and in large quantities. Bulk buying food meant less time shopping and the Magimix food processor which added a choice of blades and attachments to a standard liquidiser, made home cooking more adventurous.

IN THE 1970s

Teenage Home Entertainment

Teenagers covered their bedroom walls with posters of their favourite bands and actors, ranging from Rod Stewart and the Boomtown Rats to Olivia Newton-John and Robert Redford. The lucky ones listening to top ten singles on their own stereo record deck which had replaced the old Dansette player.

If they wanted to play the new video games, they typically went to an arcade, but in 1975, Atari PONG was released, the first commercially successful video game you could play at home on your television. Based on a simple two-dimensional graphical representation of a tennis-like game, two players used paddles to hit a ball back and forth on a black and white screen. It captivated audiences and its success influenced developers to invent more and increasingly sophisticated games for the home market.

The luxury of a Goblin Teasmade, the automatic tea-maker and alarm clock, revolutionised early morning tea.

ART AND CULTURE

1970 - 1974

1970 Laurence Olivier becomes the first actor to be made a Lord. He is given a life peerage in the Queen's Birthday Honours list.
The first Glastonbury Festival was held, called the Worthy Farm Pop Festival. About 1500 attended.

1971 Coco Chanel, the French fashion designer died. (Born 1883)
The 'Blue Peter' presenters buried a time capsule in the grounds of BBC Television Centre, due to be opened on the first episode in 2000.
Mr Tickle, the first of the Mr Men books is published.

1972 'Jesus Christ Superstar', the Tim Rice & Andrew Lloyd Webber musical opens in the West End.
John Betjeman is appointed Poet Laureate.

1973 The British Library is established by merger of the British Museum Library & the National Lending Library for Science & Technology.
Series 1 of the BBC sitcom, 'Last of the Summer Wine' begins. There are eventually, 31 series.

1974 'Tinker, Tailor, Soldier, Spy' the first of John Le Carré's novel featuring the ageing spymaster, George Smiley, is published.
The Terracotta Army of Qin Shi Huang, thousands of life-size clay models of soldiers, horses and chariots, is discovered at Xi'an in China.

Milton Keynes Shopping Centre

1975 - 1979

1975 Donald Coggan is enthroned as the Archbishop of Canterbury.
Bill Gates and Paul Allen found Microsoft in Albuquerque, New Mexico.

1976 Trevor Nunn's memorable production of 'Macbeth' opens at Stratford-upon-Avon, with Ian McKellan and Judi Dench in the lead roles.
The Royal National Theatre on the South Bank opens.
Agatha Christie's last novel, Sleeping Murder, a Miss Marple story is published posthumously.

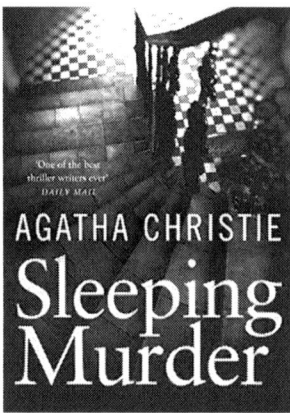

1977 Luciano Pavarotti makes his television debut singing in Puccini's La Boheme in the television debut of 'Live from the Met'.
Mike Leigh's satire on the aspirations and tastes of the new middle class emerging in the 70's, 'Abigail's Party', opened at the Hampstead Theatre starring Alison Steadman.

1978 The Andrew Lloyd Webber musical 'Evita' opens in London.
The arcade video game, 'Space Invaders' is released.

1979 Margaret Thatcher opens the new Central Milton Keynes Shopping Centre, the largest indoor shopping centre in Britain.
Anthony Blunt, British art historian and former Surveyor of the Queen's Pictures, in exposed as a double agent for the Soviets during WW2.
The Sony Walkman, portable cassette player is released.

Pavarotti at the Met.

It was in his third season at the Metropolitan Opera House in New York that Luciano Pavarotti, the operatic tenor, would skyrocket to stardom. The company imported Covent Garden's production of Donizetti's *La Fille du Régiment* in 1972 as a vehicle for Joan Sutherland. The great Australian diva enjoyed a huge triumph, but the surprise for the audience was the young Italian tenor by her side who shared an equal part in the phenomenal success. This was the historic first Met performance telecast live on PBS as part of the long-running series that continues to the present day.

The Terracotta Army

'The Qin Tomb Terracotta Warriors and Horses' was constructed between 246-206BC as an afterlife guard for China's First Emperor, Qin Shihuang, from whom, China gets its name. He ordered it built to remember the army he led to triumph over other warring states, and to unite China.

The tomb and the army were all made by hand by some 700,000 artisans and labourers, and comprises thousands of life-size soldiers, each with different facial features and expressions, clothing, hairstyles and gestures, arranged in battle array.

All figures face east, towards the ancient enemies of Qin State, in rectangular formations and three separate vaults include rows of kneeling and standing archers, chariot war configurations and mixed forces of infantry, horse drawn chariots plus numerous soldiers armed with long spears, daggers and halberds.

FILMS

1970 - 1974

1970 Love Story, was the biggest grossing film a sentimental, tearjerker with the oft-quoted tagline, "Love means never having to say you're sorry." Nominated for the Academy Awards Best Picture, it was beaten by **Patton** which won 7 major titles that year.

1971 The Oscar winner was **The French Connection** with Gene Hackman as a New York police detective, Jimmy 'Popeye' Doyle, chasing down drug smugglers. Hackman was at the peak of his career in the 70's.

1972 Francis Ford Coppola's gangster saga, **The Godfather** became the highest grossing film of its time and helped drive a resurgence in the American film industry.

1973 Glenda Jackson won Best Actress for her role in **A Touch of Class.** She revealed that she was approached for the part by the director after appearing in the 1971 'Antony & Cleopatra' sketch on the Morecambe & Wise show. After she won, Eric Morecambe sent her a telegram saying, "Stick with us and we will get you another one".

1974 New films this year included **The Godfather Part II,** which won the Oscar, **Blazing Saddles** the comedy western and the disaster film, **The Towering Inferno** starring Paul Newman and Steve McQueen.

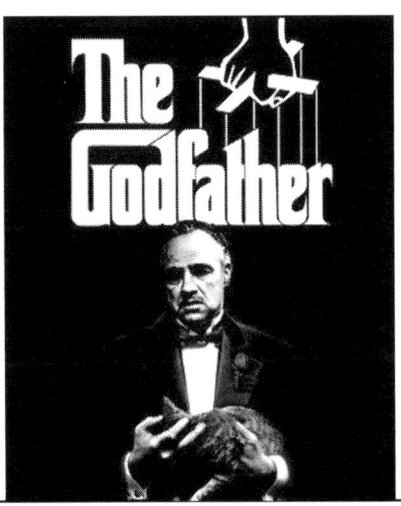

1975 - 1979

1975 One Flew Over the Cuckoo's Nest, an allegorical film set in a mental hospital, starring Jack Nicholson, beat tough competition for Best Picture from Spielberg's **Jaws** and Altman's **Nashville.**

1976 Jodi Foster won an Oscar in Martin Scorsese's gritty film **Taxi Driver** which examines alienation in urban society but it was Sylvester Stallone's **Rocky** that carried off the Best Picture award.

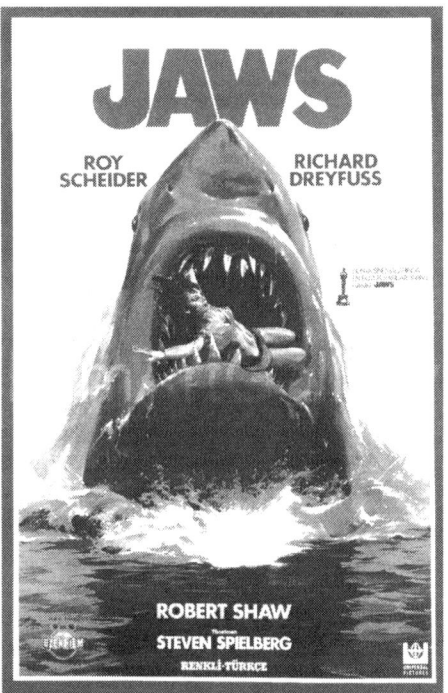

1977 Annie Hall from Woody Allen, the winner of Best Picture is a masterpiece of witty and quotable one-liners.

1978 The Vietnam War is examined through the lives of three friends from a small steel-mill town before, during and after their service in **The Deer Hunter**. A powerful and disturbing film.

1979 In this year's Best Picture, **Kramer v Kramer** there is a restaurant scene where Dustin Hoffman throws his wine glass at the wall. Only the cameraman was forewarned, Meryl Streep's shocked reaction was genuine!

Star Wars

Star Wars all began with George Lucas's eponymous film in 1977. The epic space fantasy, telling the adventures of characters "A long time ago in a galaxy far, far away", and this first film was a world beater in special effects technology using new computerised and digital effects. It rapidly became a phenomenon, Luke Skywalker, Jedi Knights, Princess Leia and Darth Vader becoming household names. An immensely valuable franchise grew up to include the films, television series, video games, books, comics and theme parks which now amounts to billions of dollars and the film introduced the phrase "May the Force be with you" into common usage.

Apocalypse Now

Joseph Conrad's book 'Heart of Darkness' was the inspiration for producer and director Francis Ford Coppola's psychological film, a metaphor for the madness and folly of war itself for a generation of young American men. Beautiful, with symbolic shots showing the confusion, violence and fear of the nightmare of the Vietnam War, much of it was filmed on location in the Philippines where expensive sets were destroyed by severe weather, a typhoon called 'Olga', Marlon Brando showed up on set overweight and completely unprepared and Martin Sheen had a near-fatal heart attack.

This led to the film being two and a half times over budget and taking twice the number of scheduled weeks to shoot. When filming finally finished, the release was postponed several times as Coppola had six hours of film to edit. The helicopter attack scene with the 'Ride of the Valkyries' soundtrack is one of the most memorable film scenes ever.

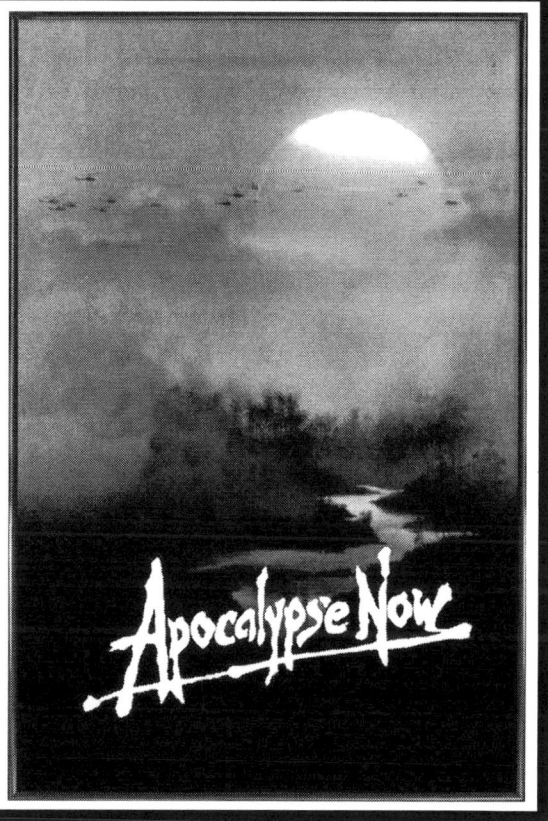

Women Wear the Trousers

It is often said that 1970s styles had no direction and were too prolific. French couture no longer handed down diktats of what we should be wearing, and the emerging street style was inventive, comfortable, practical for women or glamorous. It could be home-made, it was whatever you wanted it to be, and the big new trend was for gender neutral clothes, women wore trousers in every walk of life, trouser suits for the office, jeans at home and colourful, tight-fitting ones for in between. Trouser legs became wider and 'bell-bottoms', flared from the knee down, with bottom leg openings of up to twenty-six inches, made from denim, bright cotton and satin polyester, became mainstream. Increasingly 'low cut', they were teamed with platform soles or high cut boots until they could not flare anymore, and so, by the end of the decade they had gone, skin-tight trousers, in earth tones, greys, whites and blacks were much more in vogue.

And the Hot Pants

In the early 70s, women's styles were very flamboyant with extremely bright colours and, in the winter, long, flowing skirts and trousers *but* come the summer, come the Hot Pants. These extremely short shorts were made of luxury fabrics such as velvet and satin designed for fashionable wear, not the practical equivalents for sports or leisure, and they enjoyed great popularity until falling out of fashion in the middle of the decade. Teamed with skin-tight t-shirts, they were favourites for clubwear and principally worn by women, including Jacqueline Kennedy Onassis, Elizabeth Taylor and Jane Fonda, but they were also worn by some high-profile men, David Bowie, Sammy Davis Jnr and Liberace among them, although the shorts were slightly longer than the women's versions, but still shorter than usual. Chest hair, medallions, sideburns and strangely, tennis headbands, finished the look!

These Boots Are Made For Walking

Boots were so popular in the early 1970s that even men were getting in on the action. It wasn't uncommon to see a man sporting 2" inch platform boots inspired by John Travolta in Saturday Night Fever. The trend was all about being sexy on the dance floor!

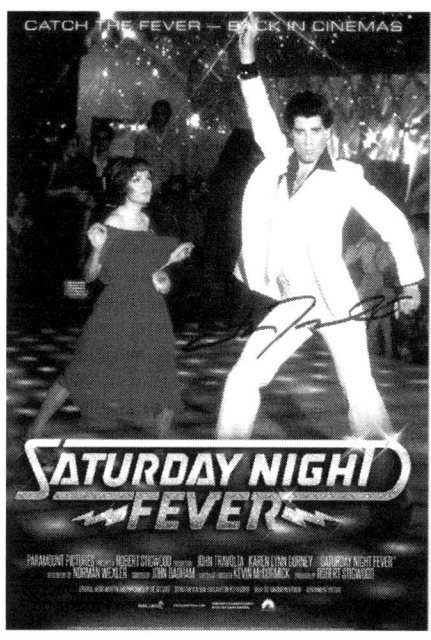

And Punk Was Not to Be Ignored

Emerging in the mid 70s in London as an anarchic and aggressive movement, a few hundred young people defined themselves as an anti-fashion urban youth street culture closely aligned to the music that became punk. They cut up old clothes from charity shops, destroyed the fabric and refashioned outfits in a manner intended to shock. Trousers were deliberately torn to reveal laddered tights and dirty legs and worn with heavy Doc Martens footwear, now seen on many young women too.

Safety pins and chains held bits of fabric together. Neck chains were made from padlocks and chain and even razor blades were used as pendants. Body piercings and studs, beginning with the three-stud earlobe, progressing to the ear outline embedded with ear studs, evolved to pins in eyebrows, cheeks, noses or lips and together with tattoos were the beginning of unisex fashion. All employed by male and female alike to offend. Vivienne Westwood and Malcolm McLaren quickened the style with her bondage shop "Sex", and his punk music group, the "Sex Pistols".

LEISURE

Saturday Morning TV

In the early 70s, Saturday mornings for many children still meant a trip to the cinema but with the advent of Saturday Morning Television, under instruction 'not to wake their parents', children could creep downstairs, switch on the box and stay entertained until lunchtime.

First, in 1974, came ITV's 'Tiswas', hosted by Chris Tarrant it was a chaotic blend of jokes, custard pies and buckets of water.

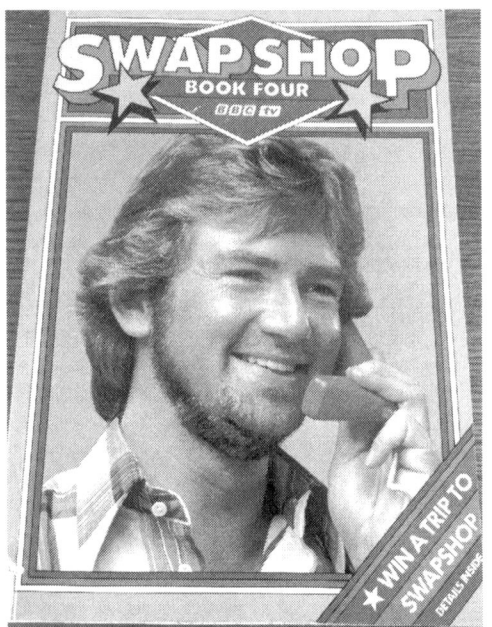

Then in 1976, the BBC introduced 'Swap Shop' with Noel Edmonds, Keith Chegwin and John Craven and a Saturday morning ritual was born. Nearly three hours of ground-breaking television using the 'phone-in' extensively for the first time on TV. The programme included music, competitions, cartoons and spontaneous nonsense from Edmonds. There was coverage of news and issues relevant to children, presented by 'Newsround's' John Craven but by far the most popular element of the show was the "Swaporama" open-air event, hosted by Chegwin. An outside broadcast unit would travel to different locations throughout the UK where sometimes as many as 2000 children would gather to swap their belongings with others.

Saturday Night Fever

Memories of Saturday night and Sunday morning in the discotheque. A mirror ball; strobe lights; 'four on the floor' rhythm; the throb of the bass drum; girls in Spandex tops with hot pants or vividly coloured, shiny, Lycra trousers with equally dazzling halter neck tops; boys in imitations of John Travolta's white suit from Saturday Night Fever risking life and limb on towering platform shoes.

These glamorous dancers, clad in glitter, metallic lame and sequins, gyrating as the music pounded out at the direction of the DJ, whirling energetically and glowing bright 'blue-white' under the ultra-violet lights as their owners 'strutted their stuff', perspiration running in rivulets down their backs.

The DJs, stars in their own right, mixed tracks by Donna Summer, the Bee Gees, Gloria Gaynor, Sister Sledge, Chic and Chaka Khan, as their sexy followers, fuelled by the night club culture of alcohol and drugs, changed from dancing the Hustle with their partners to the solo freestyle dancing of John Travolta.

The Dangers of Leisure

In the 1970's the Government was intent on keeping us all – and particularly children – safe and continued producing the wartime Public Information Films, which were still scaring children witless!

1971: Children and Disused Fridges: Graphic warnings of children being suffocated in old fridges that, tempted by their playful imaginations, they want to climb into.

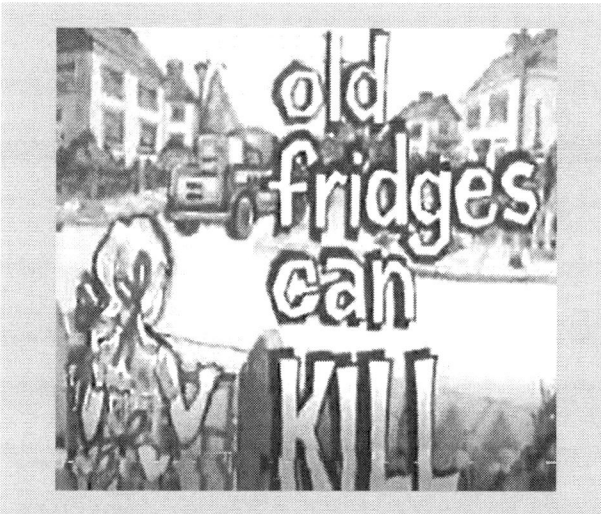

1973: Broken Glass: This film shows a boy running on the sand, ending abruptly before he steps on a broken glass bottle, the film urges people to use a bin or take their litter home with them.

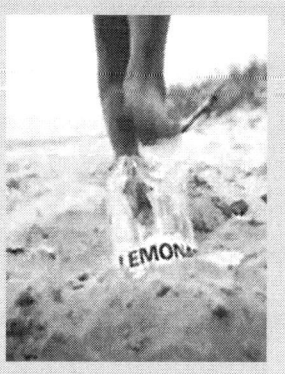

1974: The Fatal Floor: This 30 second film had the message, "Polish a floor, put a rug on it, and you might as well set a man trap..."

1979: Play Safe – Frisbee: This film used chilling electronic music and frightening sound effects to highlight the potentially fatal combination of frisbees with electricity pylons and kites, fishing rods and radio-controlled planes.

1972: Teenagers – Learn to Swim:

A cartoon aimed at teenagers warns them to learn how to swim, or risk social embarrassment and failure to attract the opposite sex. The female character's illusion of her boyfriend 'Dave' being able 'to do anything' is shattered after she wishes they were at the seaside, where she discovers Dave can't swim. He in turn wishes he didn't 'keep losing me birds' after his girlfriend disappears with 'Mike' who 'swims like a fish'. Although the film is light-hearted in tone it was intended in part to help prevent accidents.

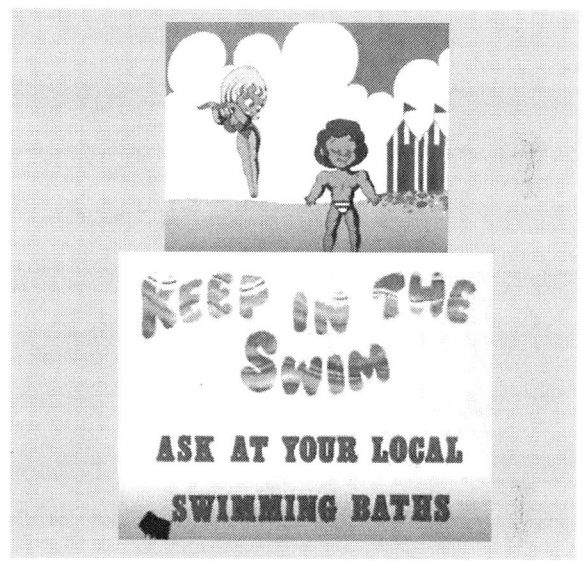

1975: Protect and Survive:

This was the title of a series of booklets and films made in the late 1970s and early 1980s, dealing with emergency planning for a nuclear war including the recognition of attack warning, fallout warning, and all-clear signals, the preparation of a home "fallout room" and the stockpiling of food, water, and other emergency supplies. In the opinion of some contemporary critics, the films *were deeply and surprisingly fatalistic in tone*!

Music

1970 - 1974

1970 Number 1 for 3 weeks, **Bridge Over Troubled Water** by Simon and Garfunkel became their 'signature song' selling over 6m copies worldwide. It also became one of the most performed songs of the 20th century, covered by over 50 artists.

1971 George Harrison's first release as a solo **My Sweet Lord** topped the charts for five weeks and became the best selling UK single of the year.
Rod Stewart had 7 No 1's this year including in October, the double sided hits, **Reason to Believe/Maggie May**

1972 A jingle, rewritten to become the hugely popular 'Buy the world a Coke' advert for the Coca Cola company, was re-recorded by The New Seekers as the full-length song, **I'd Like to Teach the World to Sing**, which stayed at No 1 for 4 weeks.

1973 Dawn featuring Tony Orlando had the bestselling single of 1973 with **"Tie a Yellow Ribbon Round the 'Ole Oak Tree"**, which spent four weeks at the top spot and lasted 11 weeks in the top ten.
Queen released their debut album, **"Queen"**. The Carpenters reached number 2 with **"Yesterday Once More"**.

1974 Waterloo, the winning song for Sweden in the Eurovision Song Contest began ABBA's journey to world-wide fame.
David Essex has his first No 1 with **Wanna Make You a Star** which spends 3 weeks at the top of the charts.

1975 - 1979

1975 Make Me Smile (Come Up and See Me) was a chart topper for Steve Harley & Cockney Rebel. **Bohemian Rhapsody** for Queen, stayed at the top for nine weeks.

1976 The Brotherhood of Man won the Eurovision Song Contest for Great Britain with **Save Your Kisses for Me**. It became the biggest-selling song of the year and remains one of the biggest-selling Eurovision winners ever.
Don't Go Breaking My Heart was the first No. 1 single in the UK for both Elton John and Kiki Dee.

1977 Actor David Soul, riding high on his success in Starsky & Hutch, had the No 1 spot for 4 weeks with **Don't Give Up on Us**.
Way Down was the last song to be recorded by Elvis Presley before his death and stayed at No 1 for 5 weeks.

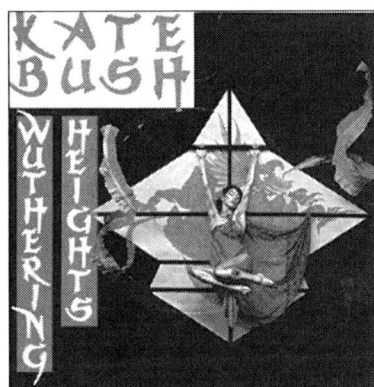

1978 Kate Bush released her debut single, **Wuthering Heights,** which she had written aged 18 after watching Emily Brontë's Wuthering Heights on television and discovering she shared the author's birthday.
Spending five weeks at the top of the British charts, Boney M's **"Rivers of Babylon"** became the biggest selling single of the year, exceeding one million sales between May and June.

1979 Frequently recalled as a symbol of female empowerment, **I Will Survive** reached the top for Gloria Gaynor.
The Wall, Pink Floyd's rock opera was released, featuring all three parts of **Another Brick in the Wall. Part 2**, written as a protest against rigid schooling was No1 in Dec.

The Decade in Numbers

Most No1 Singles:
ABBA with seven.
Waterloo (1974);
Mamma Mia, Fernando and
Dancing Queen (all 1976);
Knowing Me Knowing You, The Name of the Game, (both 1977);
Take a Chance on Me (1978).

Most Weeks at No 1:
Bohemian Rhapsody by Queen; **Mull of Kintyre / Girl's School** by Wings;
You're the One That I Want by John Travolta and Olivia Newton-John.

WINGS

MULL OF KINTYRE

'Danny' and 'Sandy' Fever

Grease, the 1978 musical romantic comedy starring John Travolta (Danny) and Olivia Newton-John (Sandy) had phenomenal success. In June to August 1978, **You're the One That I Want** and in September to October, **Summer Nights**, locked up the number 1 position for a total of sixteen weeks.

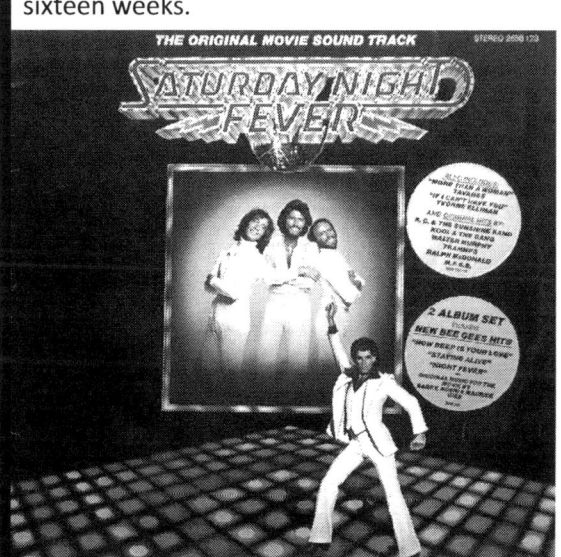

Hopelessly Devoted to You was nominated for an Oscar and John Travolta and Olivia Newton-John seemed to be constantly in the public conscience. Critically and commercially successful, the soundtrack album ended 1978 as the second best -selling album in the US, behind the soundtrack of the 1977 blockbuster **Saturday Night Fever,** which also starred John Travolta.

SCIENCE AND NATURE

Pocket Calculators

The first pocket calculators came onto the market towards the end of 1970. In the early 70s they were an expensive status symbol but by the middle of the decade, businessmen were quite used to working their sales figures out quickly whilst 'out of the office'.

Household accounts were made easy and children wished they could use them at school – not just to help with homework. Most early calculators performed only basic addition, subtraction, multiplication and division but the speed and accuracy, sometimes giving up to 12 digit answers, of the machine proved sensational.

In 1972, Hewlett Packard introduced the revolutionary HP-35 pocket calculator which, in addition to the basic operations, enabled advanced mathematical functions. It was the first scientific, hand-held calculator, able to perform a wide number of logarithmic and trigonometric functions, store intermediate solutions and utilise scientific notations.

With intense competition, prices of pocket calculators dropped rapidly, and the race was on to produce the smallest possible models. The target was to be no bigger than a credit card. Casio won the race.

The Miracle of IVF

In 1971, Patrick Steptoe, gynaecologist, Robert Edwards, biologist, and Jean Purdy, nurse and embryologist set up a small laboratory at the Kershaw's Hospice in Oldham which was to lead to the development of in vitro fertilisation and eventual birth of Louise Brown in 1978.

They developed a technique for retrieving eggs at the right time and fertilising them in the laboratory, believing that they could be implanted back in the uterus. It took more than 80 embryo transfers before the first successful pregnancy, and the birth of Louise, the first 'test-tube baby', heralded the potential happiness of infertile people and a bright future for British science andindustry.

IN THE 1970s

"Houston We Have a Problem"

In April 1970, two days after the launch of Apollo 13, the seventh crewed mission in the Apollo space program and the third meant to land on the Moon, the NASA ground crew heard the now famous message, "Houston, we've had a problem." An oxygen tank had exploded, and the lunar landing was aborted leaving the astronauts in serious danger. The crew looped around the Moon and returned safely to Earth, their safe return being down to the ingenuity under pressure by the crew, commanded by Jim Lovell, together with the flight controllers and mission control. The crew experienced great hardship, caused by limited power, a chilly and wet cabin and a shortage of drinking water.

Even so, Apollo 13 set a spaceflight record for the furthest humans have travelled from Earth.

Tens of millions of viewers watched Apollo 13 splashdown in the South Pacific Ocean and the recovery by USS Iwo Jima.

The global campaigning network **Greenpeace** was founded in 1971 by Irving and Dorothy Stowe, environmental activists. The network now has 26 independent national or regional organisations in 55 countries worldwide.

Their stated goal is to ensure the ability of the earth to nurture life in all its diversity. To achieve this they "use non-violent, creative confrontation to expose global environmental problems, and develop solutions for a green and peaceful future". In detail to:

- Stop the planet from warming beyond 1.5° in order to prevent the most catastrophic impacts of the climate breakdown.
- Protect biodiversity in all its forms.
- Slow the volume of hyper-consumption and learn to live within our means.
- Promote renewable energy as a solution that can power the world.
- Nurture peace, global disarmament and non-violence.

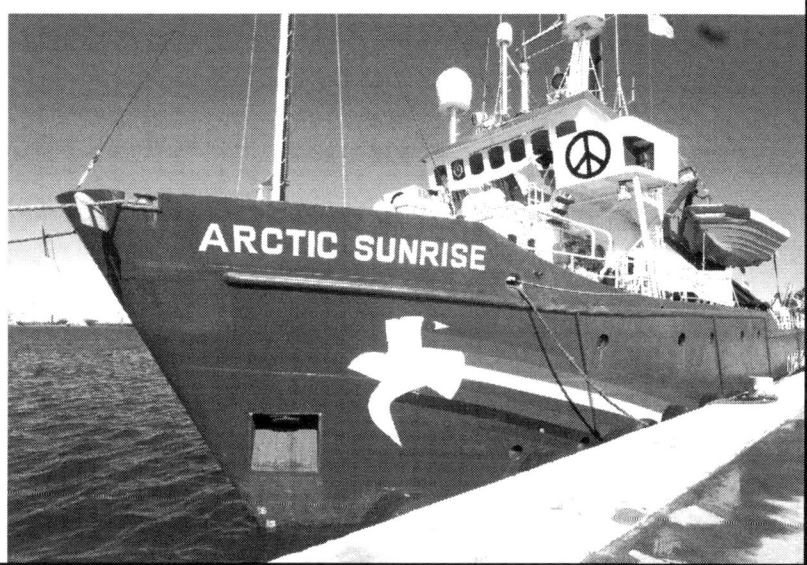

SPORT

1970 - 1974

1970 The thoroughbred 'Nijinsky', wins all three English Triple Crown Races: **The 2,000 Guineas** at Newmarket; **The Derby** at Epsom; the **St. Leger Stakes** at Doncaster and the Irish Derby. The first horse to do this in 35 years and not repeated as of 2021.

1971 Arsenal wins both the **First Division** title and the **FA Cup**, becoming the fourth team ever to win the double.
Jack Nicklaus wins his ninth major at the **PGA Championship**, the first golfer ever to win all four majors for the second time.

1972 At **Wimbledon**, Stan Smith (US) beat Ilie Nastase in the Men's Singles Final. It was his only Wimbledon title.
In the Women's Final, Billie Jean King (US) beat Yvonne Goolagong (AUS) to gain her fourth **Wimbledon** title.
The **Olympic Games** held in Munich are overshadowed by the murder of eleven Israeli athletes and coaches by Palestinian Black September members.

1973 George Foreman knocks out Joe Frazier in only two rounds to take the **World Heavyweight Boxing** Championship title.

Red Rum wins the **Grand National** with a new record and staging a spectacular comeback on the run-in having trailed the leader by 15 lengths at the final fence.

1974 Liverpool win the **FA Cup Final** against Newcastle United at Wembley. Kevin Keegan scored two of their three goals.
Eddie Merckx wins the **Tour de France**, becoming the first rider to win the Triple Crown of Cycling, **Tour de France**, **Giro d'Italia** and **World Championships** in one calendar year.

1975 - 1979

1975 In athletics, John Walker (NZ) sets a new world record becoming the first man to **run a mile** in under 3 mins 50 seconds. He clocks 3mins 49.4 secs.
Muhammad Ali defeats Joe Frazier in the 'Thrilla In Manilla' to maintain the **Boxing Heavyweight Championship** of the world.

1976 The **Olympics** are held in Montreal. Britain's only medal is a Bronze, won by Brendan Foster running the **10,000 metres**.
John Curry, becomes the **European, Olympic and World Figure Skating Champion**. He was the first skater to combine, ballet and modern dance into his skating.

1977 The commercial **World Series Cricket** was introduced by Kerry Packer. WSC changed the nature of the game with its emphasis on the "gladiatorial" aspect of fast bowling and heavy promotion of fast bowlers.

1978 During the **Oxford and Cambridge Boat Race,** the Cambridge boat sinks. It is the first sinking in the race since 1951.
Wales wins the rugby **Five Nations Championship** and completes the Grand Slam having beaten England, France, Ireland and Scotland.

1978 Arsenal beat Manchester United 3-2 in the **FA Cup Final.**
At **The Open** at Royal Lytham & St Annes Golf Club Seve Ballesteros becomes the first golfer from Continental Europe to win a major since 1907.

IN THE 1970s

Traffic Lights and Football

Before the introduction of Red and Yellow Cards in football, cautions or sending a player off had to be dealt with orally, and the language barrier could sometimes present problems. For example, in the 1966 World Cup, the German referee tried in vain to send Argentinian player Antonio Rattin off the field, but Rattin did not 'want' to understand and eventually was escorted off the pitch by the police! Ken Aston, Head of World Cup Referees, was tasked with solving this problem and legend has it that the idea of the red and yellow cards came to him when he was stopped in his car at traffic lights. They were tested in the 1968 Olympics and the 1970 World Cup in Mexico and introduced to European leagues soon after and after six years, to English football.

In 1976, the first player to be sent off using a red card in an English game was Blackburn Rovers winger David Wagstaffe.

Tour de France

In 1974 the Tour de France covered 2,546 miles in 22 stages, one of which was the first to be held in the UK, a circuit stage on the Plympton By-pass near Plymouth. Eddy Merckx of Belgium won eight stages and won the race overall with a comfortable margin, making it five wins for him out of his five Tours. He also won that year's Combination Classification – the General (Yellow Jersey), Points or Sprint (Green Jersey) and Mountains (since 1975, King of the Mountains wears the Polka Dot Jersey).

Rockstar and Racing Driver

James Hunt, the charismatic, play-boy darling of the press in the 1970's, began his Formula 1 career at the beginning of the decade with the Hesketh Racing team and gave them their only win in 1975 at the Dutch GP. He moved to McLaren in 1976, and in his first year with them, he and his great rival Niki Lauda at Ferrari, fought an epic season-long battle. It was an extraordinarily dramatic season, over sixteen races filled with drama and controversy, where Lauda had gained an early championship lead. By the final race in Japan, he was being reeled-in by Hunt and was only three points ahead. Hunt drove the race of his life, in the worst possible weather conditions, to finish in third place. Lauda, already badly injured from the crash at Nürburgring in August, withdrew because of the hazardous conditions which meant James Hunt became World Champion, winning by just a single point.

Hunt's natural driving ability was phenomenal, and while his habit of risk-taking didn't always endear him to others, hence the nickname "Hunt the Shunt", it also made him compelling to watch. Off track, he and Niki had an enduring friendship, which lasted after James's retirement from F1 in 1979 until his untimely death from a heart attack in 1993, aged just 45.

TRANSPORT

ICONIC MACHINES OF THE DECADE

The Jumbo Jet
Entered service on January 22, 1970. The 747 was the first airplane dubbed a "Jumbo Jet", the first wide-body airliner.

In 1971 Ford launched the car that was to represent the 1970s, the Cortina Mk III. In 1976 the Mk IV and 1979 Mk V. Cortinas were the best-selling cars of the decade.

The best-selling foreign import was the Datsun Sunny, which was only the 19th best-selling car of the decade.

In 1973, British Leyland's round, dumpy shaped Allegro was not at all popular and meagre sales contributed greatly to BL's collapse in 1975.

Raleigh Chopper
Shot to fame in the 70's when every child, and some adults, wanted one. It had a high back, long seat and motorbike rear wheel and was probably the first bike to have a centrally positioned gear shift.

Women Drivers

In 1974, Jill Viner became the first female bus driver for London Transport. She trained to become a bus driver at a centre in Chiswick in 1974, when London Transport were said to be 3,200 drivers short
While women had previously driven buses within bus depots during the Second World War, Viner was the first women to drive a bus in service in London. In the weeks after she started driving, it was reported that thirty women had applied to become bus drivers.

In 1978, Hannah Dadds completed a seven-week training course to qualify as a train driver and became the first female driver on the London Underground.
Hannah's sister Edna also joined the London Underground working first as a guard and then a driver. Hannah and Edna became the first all-female crew on the London Underground.

Concorde

The Anglo-French supersonic passenger airliner had a take-off speed of 220 knots (250mph) and a cruising speed of 1350mph – more than twice the speed of sound. With seating for 92 to 128 passengers, Concorde entered service in 1976 and operated for 27 years.
Twenty aircraft were built in total, including six prototypes and in the end, only Air France and British Airways purchased and flew them, due in great part to supersonic flights being restricted to ocean-crossing routes, to prevent sonic boom disturbance over land and populated areas. Concorde flew regular transatlantic flights from London and Paris to New York, Washington, Dulles in Virginia and Barbados and the BA Concorde made just under 50,000 flights and flew more than 2.5m passengers supersonically.

A typical London to New York crossing would take a little less than three and a half hours as opposed to about eight hours for a subsonic flight.

The aircraft was retired in 2003, three years after the crash of an Air France flight in which all passengers and crew were killed.

THE MAJOR NEWS STORIES

1980 - 1984

1980:

May: Mount St. Helens experiences a huge eruption that creates avalanches, explosions, large ash clouds, mudslides, and massive damage. 57 people are killed.

Dec: John Lennon, the former Beatle, age 40, is shot and killed by an obsessed fan in Manhattan.

1981:

July: Prince Charles marries Lady Diana Spencer at St Paul's Cathedral.

Margaret Thatcher's Government begins the privatisation of the Nationalised Industries.

1982:

Apr: Argentina invades the Falkland Islands and the UK retakes possession of them by the end of June.

May: Pope John Paul II visits the United Kingdom. It is the first visit by a reigning Pope

1983:

Apr: The £1 coin is introduced in the UK.

Jun: Margaret Thatcher wins a landslide victory for the Conservatives in the General Election, with a majority of 144.

Nov: The first United States cruise missiles arrive at RAF Greenham Common in Berkshire

1984:

Mar: The National Mineworkers Union led by Arthur Scargill, begin what will be a year-long strike against the National Coal Board's plans to shut 20 collieries

May: The Thames Barrier, designed to protect London from floods, is opened by9The Queen

1980: Mount St. Helens before and after the eruption. The top third of the mountain was blown away.

1982: EPCOT opened at Disney World in Florida, "...an experimental prototype community of tomorrow that will take its cue from the new ideas and technologies that are now emerging … a showcase of the ingenuity and imagination of American free enterprise." - *Walt Disney*

1984: On 31 October, Indira Gandhi, Prime Minister of India, was killed by her Sikh bodyguards.
The assassination sparked four days of riots that left more than 8,000 Indian Sikhs dead in revenge attacks.

1985 - 1989

1985: On 1st January, Ernie Wise made the first, civilian, mobile phone call in the UK from outside the Dicken's Inn at St Katharine's Dock. Via the Vodafone network he called their office in Newbury on a VT1 which weighed 5.5kg.

1987: Oct 15th: Weather-man Michael Fish: "Earlier on today, a woman rang the BBC and said she heard there was a hurricane on the way... well, if you're watching, don't worry, there isn't!". That night, hurricane force winds hit much of the South of England killing 23 people, bringing down an estimated 15 million trees and causing damage estimated at £7.3 billion.

1985:

Jan: The Internet's Domain Name System is created and the country code top-level domain .uk is registered in July.

Dec: The original charity "Comic Relief" is launched by Richard Curtis and Lenny Henry on Christmas Day,.

1986:

Apr: A Soviet Nuclear reactor at Chernobyl explodes causing the release of radioactive material across much of Europe.

Oct: The 'Big Bang' – the London Stock Exchange is deregulated allowing computerised share dealing.

1987:

Jan: Terry Waite, the special envoy of the Archbishop of Canterbury in Lebanon, is kidnapped in Beirut. He is held in captivity for 1,763 days until 1991.

Oct: Black Monday: Wall Street crash leads to £50,000,000,000 being wiped of the value of shares on the London stock exchange.

1988:

Dec: Suspected Libyan terrorist bomb explodes on Pan Am jet over Lockerbie in Scotland on December 21st killing all 259 on board and 11 on the ground.

Dec: Health Minister Edwina Currie states that most of Britain's egg production is infected with salmonella, causing an immediate nationwide slump in egg sales.

1989:

Apr: 94 fans are killed in the Hillsborough football stadium collapse in Sheffield. 3 more will die and over 300 are hospitalised.

Nov: The Fall of the Berlin Wall heralds the end of the Cold War and communism in East and Central Europe.

A Busier Life

In the 1980's, life became more stressful, there were two recessions, divorce rates were increasing, women were exercising their rights and these years were the beginning of the end of the traditional family unit. With single parent families or both parents at work and a generally 'busier' life, there was a fundamental change to the family and home. There was also a lot more choice.

Many more 'lower cost' restaurants, chilled ready-made meals, instant foods such as Findus Crispy Pancakes, Pot Noodles or M&S Chicken Kievs and the, by now, ubiquitous tea bag, together with the consumer boom in electrical labour-saving devices from food processors and microwaves to dishwashers and automatic washing machines, sandwich toasters and jug kettles, all added up to more free time from housework and cooking.

Floral Décor

Flower patterns were all the rage in early 1980s home décor, with flower patterned upholstery and curtains to floral wallpapers taking over from the 70s woodchip paper.

Artex was still hugely popular on ceilings and walls, finished with the familiar stippled or swirled patterns and peach was *the* fashionable colour of choice for interior design schemes. Chintz curtains could have more layers, swags and tails than an onion! The bold reached the height of fashion with a red and black colour scheme, black ash furniture and a framed Ferrari print on the wall – with a bold wallpaper border at the ceiling which often clashed with the paper on the walls.

The Telephone Answering Machine

There once was a time when, to use a telephone, both people had to be on the phone at the same time. You had to pick up the phone when it rang. The answering machine, one cassette tape for the outgoing message and one to record incoming calls, changed all that. By allowing people to take calls when they were away and respond to any message at a later time.

Children's Playtime

For children, toys of the early 80s had a bit of a 70s feel, Star Wars action figures, remote controlled cars and trucks, Barbie dolls and Action Men, but by 1983 there was a huge increase in toys like Transformers, Care Bears, a plethora of talking robot toys, My Little Pony, Teenage Mutant Ninja Turtles and Cabbage Patch Kids which was THE craze of 1983 – these odd looking 'little people' were the first images to feature on disposable 'designer' nappies!

Basic Atari video games evolved to Nintendo's NES game system and all of them competed with Apple and Sinclair home computers and personal Walkman stereos.

ART AND CULTURE

1980 - 1984

1980 "Who shot J.R.?" was an advertising catchphrase that CBS created to promote their TV show, 'Dallas', referring to the cliff hanger of the finale of the previous season. The episode, 'Who Done It?' aired in November with an estimated 83 million viewers tuning in.

MV Mi Amigo, the ship 'Radio Caroline', the pirate radio station, operates from, runs aground and sinks off Sheerness.

1981 A bronze statue of Charlie Chaplin, as his best loved character, The Tramp, is unveiled in Leicester Square.

1982 The D'Oyly Carte Opera Company gives its last performance at the end of a final London season, having been in near-continuous existence since 1875.

1983 Children's ITV is launched in Britain as a new branding for the late afternoon programming block on the ITV network.

1984 The comedian Tommy Cooper collapses and dies on stage from a heart attack during a live televised show, 'Live from Her Majesty's'.

Ted Hughes is appointed Poet Laureate and succeeds Sir John Betjeman. Philip Larkin had turned down the post.

1985 - 1989

1985 The Roux Brothers' Waterside Inn at Bray, Berkshire becomes the first establishment in the UK to be awarded three Michelin stars.

'Live Aid' pop concerts in London and Philadelphia raise over £50,000,000 for famine relief in Ethiopia.

1986 The Sun newspaper alleges that comedian Freddie Starr ate a live hamster.

More than 30m viewers watched the Christmas Day episode of 'East Enders' in which Den Watts serves the divorce papers on his wife Angie.

1987 Christie's auction house in London sells one of Vincent van Gogh's iconic Sunflowers paintings for £24,750,000 after a bidding war between two unidentified competitors bidding via telephone.

'The Simpsons' cartoon first appears as a series of animated short films on the 'Tracey Ullman Show' in the US.

1988 Salman Rushdie published 'The Satanic Verses' a work of fiction which caused a widespread furore and forced Rushdie to live in hiding out of fear for his life.

1989 Sky Television begins broadcasting as the first satellite TV service in Britain.

Remains of both The Rose, an Elizabethan playhouse, and the Globe Theatre are found in London.

The Great Musical Revival

By the start of the 1980's, Britain was in recession and the West End Theatres were facing rising costs and falling audiences – until the revival of the Musical, led by Andrew Lloyd Webber.

In 1981, his first 'unlikely' musical **Cats** led by Elaine Paige, went on to be the first 'megamusical' spectacular in the West End and on Broadway.

It was followed in 1984 by **Starlight Express.**

By now, these shows were being enjoyed not only by home audiences but also, a massive 44% of tickets, were purchased by tourists.

In 1986, the **Phantom of the Opera** opened to overwhelmingly positive reviews.

In 1987 **Les Misérables** brought the Royal Shakespeare Company 's expertise in high drama to the musical which was set amidst the French Revolution and brought fame to its writers, Alain Boubill and Claude-Michel Schönberg fame and producer Cameron Mackintosh his millions.

Other hit musicals of the decade: Willy Russel's **Blood Brothers**, Noël Gay's revival of **Me and My Girl**, and Lloyd Webber's **Aspects of Love.**

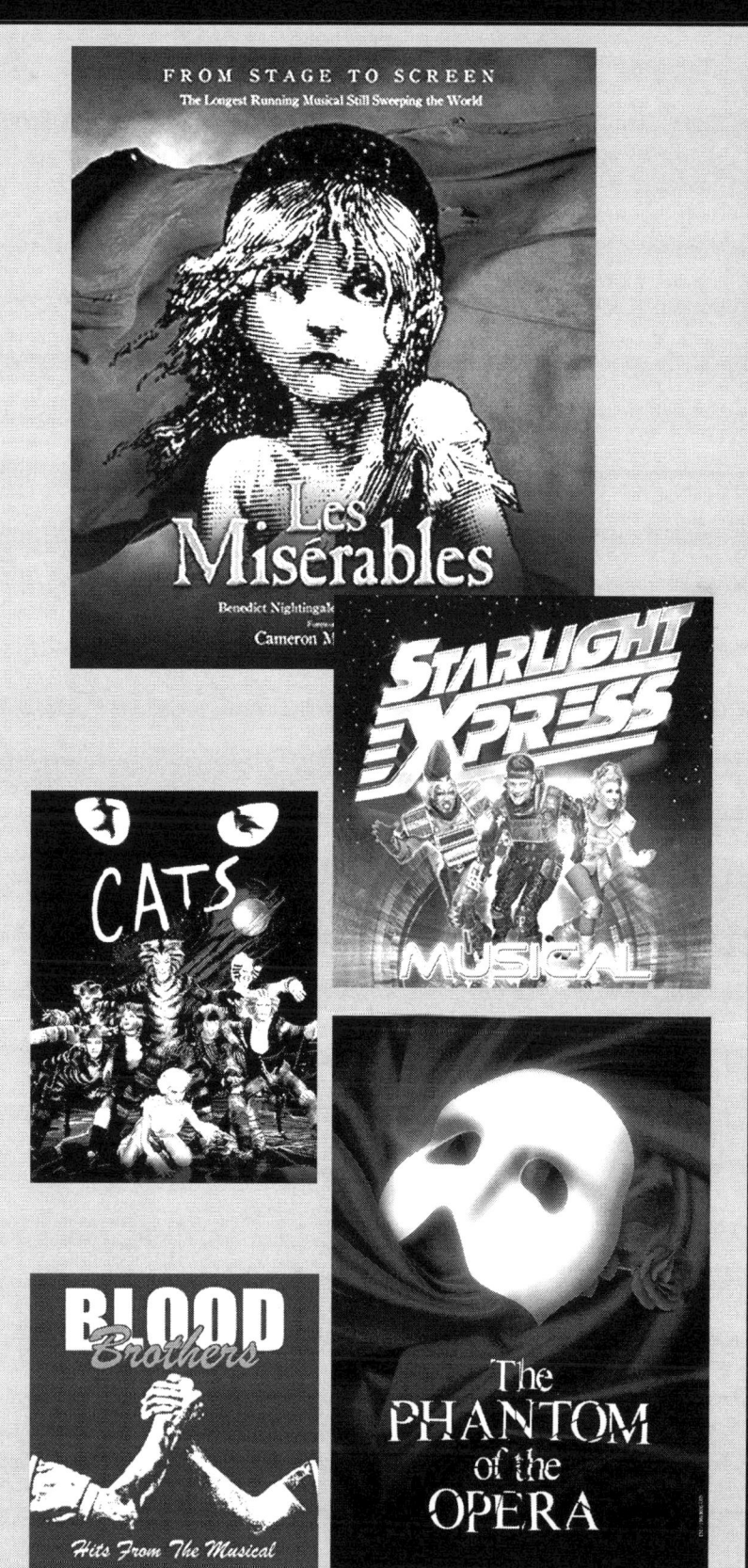

1980 - 1984

1980 The epic **The Empire Strikes Back** is released and is the highest-grossing film of the year, just as its predecessor, **Star Wars** was in 1977. However, the Oscar for Best Picture went to **Ordinary People**, the psychological drama depicting the disintegration of an upper middle-class family in Illinois.

1981 Chariots of Fire based on the true story of two British athletes, one Christian, one Jewish in the 1924 Olympics, won the Academy Awards.
The film's title was inspired by the line "Bring me my Chariot of fire!" from Blake's poem adapted as the hymn 'Jerusalem'.

1982 Spielberg's science fiction film of **ET the Extra Terrestrial** was a huge box office hit this year, the scene when the little green extra-terrestrial learns to speak, instilled "ET phone home" into the collective memory. The rather more down to earth biographical film of Mahatma Gandhi **Gandhi**, picked up the Best Film award.

 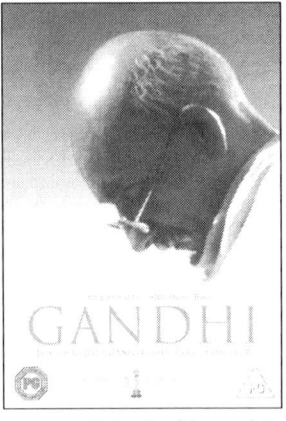

1983 There were many great British films this year including **Local Hero** and **Educating Rita, The Dresser** and Sean Connery playing Bond for the last time in **Never Say Never Again.** It was the American, **Terms of Endearment** that won the Oscars.

1984 Amadeus the fictionalised story of the composer Wolfgang Amadeus Mozart and a supposed rivalry with Italian composer Antonio Salieri, featuring much of Mozart's music, won the imagination of the audiences and the Best Film of the Year award too.

1985 - 1989

1985 Spielberg's 'coming of age' epic starring Whoopi Goldberg in her breakthrough role, **The Color Purple**, was nominated for eleven Academy Awards but failed to achieve a single win. The prize went to Meryl Streep and Robert Redford in the romantic drama, **Out of Africa.**

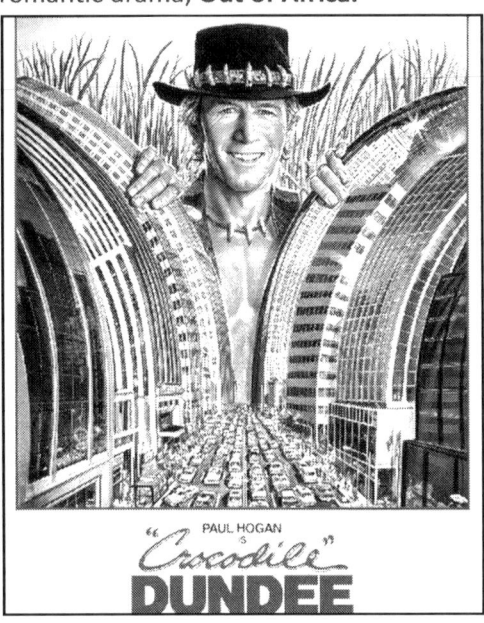

1986 The first of Oliver Stone's trilogy based on his experiences in the Vietnam war, **Platoon** picks up this year's Oscar for Best Film, beating two British nominations, **A Room with a View** and **The Mission.** This was also the year of the Australian box office runaway success, **Crocodile Dundee.**

1987 The thriller **Fatal Attraction** attracted both favourable reviews and controversy. It put the phrase 'bunny boiler' into the urban dictionary.

1988 Glenn Close was nominated for Best Actress for her role as the Marquise de Merteuil who plots revenge against her ex-lover, in **Dangerous Liaisons.** Dustin Hoffman and Tom Cruise starred in **Rainman**, the winner of Best Film of the year.

1989 Unusually, it was a PG rated film, **Driving Miss Daisy** that won the Academy Award this year, a gentle, heartwarming comedy which had the serious themes of racism and anti-semitism at its heart. Jessica Tandy at age 81, won Best Actress, the oldest winner to do so.

David Puttnam, Baron Puttnam of Queensgate (1997)

The 1980s saw the release of several films by the British producer, David Puttnam, beginning with, in 1981, his most successful film up until that time, **Chariots of Fire**.

His next big success was **Local Hero** the comedy drama, set on the west coast of Scotland where an American oil company wishes to purchase a local village and surrounding area.
Next, in 1984, came the acclaimed **Cal**, a young man on the fringes of the IRA who falls in love with a Catholic woman whose husband, a Protestant policeman, had been killed by the IRA one year earlier. Entered into the Cannes Film Festival, Helen Mirren won Best Actress.

Also in 1984, Puttnam produced **The Killing Fields**, a harrowing biographical drama about the Khmer Rouge in Cambodia, based on the experiences of a Cambodian journalist and an American journalist. This film received seven Oscar nominations and won three, most notably Best Supporting Actor for Haing S. Ngor who had no previous acting experience.

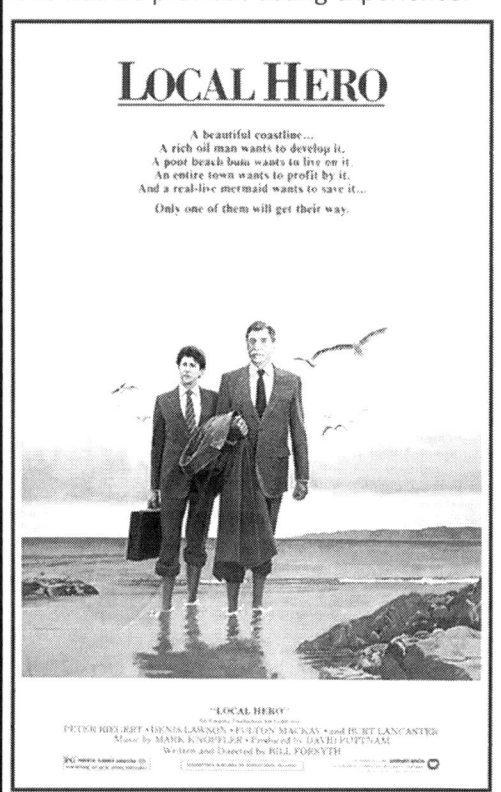

Puttnam's career spanned the 1960s to the 1990s and his films have won 10 Oscars, 31 BAFTAs, 13 Golden Globes, nine Emmys, four David di Donatellos in Italy and the Palme d'Or at Cannes.

FASHION

A Fashion Statement

The mid to late 80s was the time to 'make a statement'. The mass media took over fashion trends completely and fashion magazines, TV shows and music videos all played a part in dictating the latest bold fashions.

There was a huge emphasis on bright colours, huge shoulder pads, power suits which gave an exaggerated silhouette like an upside-down triangle, flashy skirts and spandex leggings, velour, leg warmers and voluminous parachute pants.

We wore iconic oversized plastic hoop earrings, rubber bracelets and shiny chain necklaces and huge sunglasses giving faces the appearance of large flies. Men and women alike made their hair 'big' with or without the ubiquitous teased perm and for the girls, glossy pink lips, overly filled-in brows, rainbow-coloured eye shadows and exaggerated blusher were on trend.

Men too joined in with style and sported oversized blazers with shiny buttons, pinstripe two-piece suits and sweaters, preferably from Ralph Lauren, draped over the shoulders.

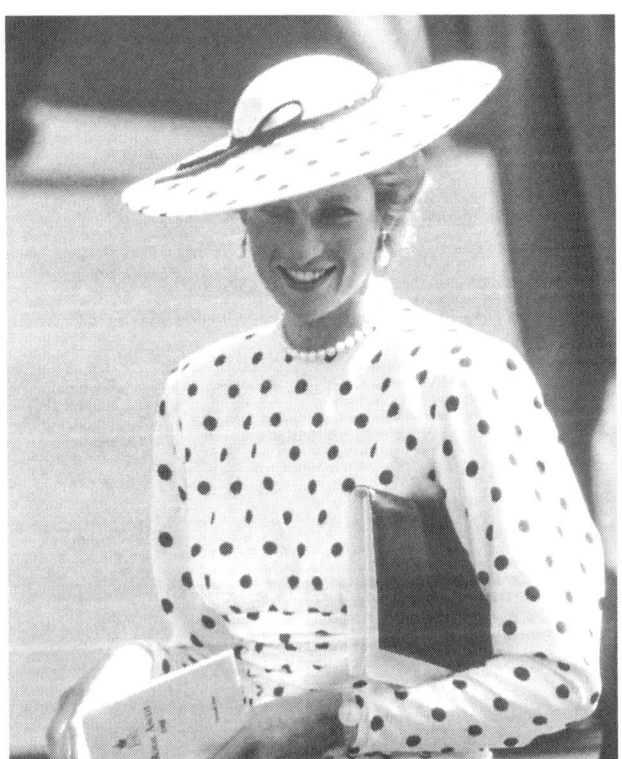

Polka Dots

Although not new to the 80s - Disney's Minnie Mouse was first seen in the 1920's wearing the red and white dottie print - polka dots were also very popular.

Bands such as The Beat used them in their music videos and well-known celebrities including Madonna and Princess Diana loved the cool look of polka dot dresses and tops.

When teamed with the oversized earrings of the decade and big hair, whilst bucking the trend for bright, gaudy colours, they still "made a statement".

Carolina Herrera used polka dots on most of her dresses during the late 1980s and early 1990s and it remains a key print in her collections, a classic.

As Marc Jacobs, the American designer famously said, "There is never a wrong time for a polka dot."

Labels, logos and idols

Pale blue, distressed jeans were the fashionable 'street wear', worn semi fitted and held with a statement belt at the natural waistline. When the boy band Bros came along in 1988, wearing jeans ripped at the knee coupled with leather, slip on loafers, teens up and down the country enthusiastically took the scissors to their own jeans, and ripped, frayed or shredded them.

.

Pop Fashion
If you were into pop music in the 1980s, there's no doubt that superstar Madonna influenced what you wore.

Feet also presented a branding opportunity, Patrick Cox had celebrities make his loafers universally desired, and, often credited with kicking off the whole fashion sneaker movement, Nike Air 'Jordans' – named after basketball star, Michael Jordan – were launched in 1985. If you couldn't have them, then high-top Reebok sneakers were also the pinnacle of style -- as were Adidas Superstar kicks and matching tracksuits.

The Fitness Craze

The 1980's had a fitness craze. Celebrities made aerobics videos and endorsed weight loss products and equipment. Health Clubs and Gyms became the place to be and to be seen but were predominantly for men so for women who wanted to exercise in the privacy of their own home, by the mid '80s, there were very few households that didn't own at least one well-worn VHS copy of **'Jane Fonda's Workout'**.

Her 1982 video sold more than 17 million copies, with the actress wearing a striped and belted leotard, violet leggings and leg warmers, big, big hair and in full make-up and working up a sweat to some heavy synth music, inspired a whole generation.

At home, between 1983 and 1987, Britain's answer to Jane Fonda, Diana Moran **'The Green Goddess',** appeared on TV screens wearing her trade-mark green leotard telling millions of BBC Breakfast viewers to 'wake up and shape up' with her aerobics routines.

What's On Telly?

Television was a very large part of leisure in the 1980s and with the massive growth in video recorders, the whole family had more control over what they watched and when they watched it.

It was the decade when the huge American 'soaps' **Dallas** and **Dynasty** dominated the ratings and influenced popular debate as well as fashions. In Britain there was a rash of police dramas and the introduction of female detectives in both BBC **'Juliet Bravo'** and ITV **'The Gentle Touch'**. They also covered the land, **'Taggart'** in Scotland, **'Bergerac'** in Jersey, **'The Chinese Detective'** in London and **'Inspector Morse'** in Oxford.

Channel 4 launched in 1982 with its first programme being **'Countdown',** Breakfast TV began in 1983, in 1980s television produced 'historic' shared experiences, **'Who Shot JR'** in Dallas watched by 80 million, the finale of **MASH**, 'Goodbye, Farewell and Amen', by more than 100 million, 30 million tuned in to watch 'Dirty Den' serve his wife 'Angie' with the divorce papers in East Enders and 27 million watched the episode after Alan Bradley tried to kill Rita Fairclough in **Coronation Street**.

What Was New?

Whilst the 80s made huge advances in technology for leisure, Game Boy and Nintendo, VCRs and CDs, disposable cameras and brick shaped mobile phones too, there were other innovations.

In this decade of high disposable income and the first credit cards, we were spending on BMX bikes, Trivial Pursuit and Rubik's Cubes.

Nike told us to 'Just Do It' and we wondered how we'd ever managed without Post-It Notes and disposable contact lenses.

What the world did not want however, was New Coke. Coca Cola changed their classic formula for a sweeter one which received an extremely poor response.

It was one of the worst marketing blunders ever because for the public, this tampered recipe 'Just wasn't it!'. The company brought back the original Coke and sold this new formula as the 'New Coke' till the early 90s.

MUSIC

1980 - 1984

1980 Johnny Logan won the Eurovision Song Contest for Ireland with **What's Another Year** and was No 1 in the UK charts for two weeks in May. He won again in 1987 with **Hold Me Now**.
Abba had their first No 1 of the year with **Winner Takes it All** followed in November with **Super Trouper.**

1981 Two singles stayed at the top of the charts for 5 weeks each this year. First Adam and the Ants with **Stand and Deliver** and in December, The Human League with **Don't You Want Me** which was also the best-selling single of the year.

1982 The year's best seller was Dexey's Midnight Runners and **Come on Eileen**, their second No 1 in the UK. The words express the feelings of an adolescent dreaming of being free from the strictures of a Catholic society and sounded unlike the other hits of the era, no synthesiser, but a banjo, accordion, fiddle and saxophone.

1983 Karma Chameleon by the 'New Romantic' band, Culture Club, fronted by singer Boy George, whose androgynous style of dressing caught the attention of the public and the media, became the second Culture Club single to reach No 1 and stayed there for six weeks, also becoming the best-selling single of the year.

1984 Two Tribes, the anti-war song by the Liverpool band, Frankie Goes to Hollywood, was a phenomenal success helped by a wide range of remixes and supported by an advertising campaign depicting the band as members of the Red Army. It entered the charts at No 1 and stayed there for nine consecutive weeks, making it the the longest-running No 1 single of the decade.

1985 - 1989

1985 The best seller this year was **The Power of Love** sung by Jennifer Rush. No 1 for five weeks, Rush became the first female artist ever to have a million-selling single in the UK.
Wham and George Michael, having had three No 1's last year, **Wake Me Up Before You Go-Go, Careless Whisper** and **Freedom**, managed only one this year, **I'm Your Man.**

1986 Holiday disco songs such as **Agadoo**, topped the charts for three weeks.
The Christmas No 1 spot was held for four weeks by a reissue, three years after his death, of Jackie Wilson's **Reet Petite (The Sweetest Girl in Town)**.

1987 Two singles stayed at No 1 for five weeks, the best-selling of the year, **Never Gonna Give You Up** by Rick Astley and **China in Your Hand** by T'Pau, Carol Decker's group named after the character in Star Trek.

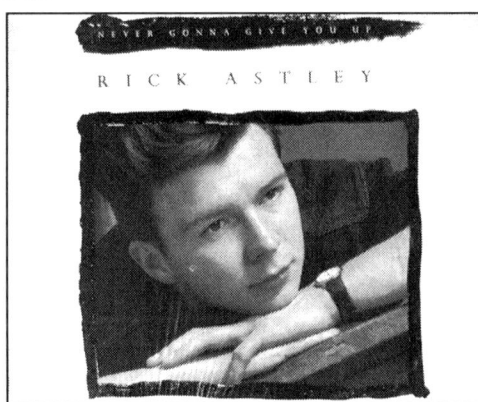

1988 Already known from the Australian soap opera, 'Neighbours', Kylie Minogue burst into the UK charts with **I Should Be So Lucky** from her debut studio album. The song became a worldwide hit.
Cliff Richard was back at No 1 after quite a break, with **Mistletoe and Wine** for the Christmas market.

1989 It was a good year for the Australian golden couple, Jason Donovan and Kylie Minogue. One No 1 together, **Especially For You,** two for Jason, **Too Many Broken Hearts** and **Sealed With a Kiss**, and one for Kylie, **Hand on Your Heart.**
Ride on Time from the debut album by Italian house music group, Black Box, topped the charts for six weeks and sold the most copies of the year.

Charity Fund Raisers

The 80's saw many 'not for profit' Charity Singles, the best-known being Bob Geldorf and Midge Ure's 'Band Aid' and then 'Live Aid', formed to raise money for famine relief in Ethiopia, who released **Do They Know Its Christmas**, for the first time, in December 1984. It stayed at the top of the charts for five weeks and was the best-selling record of the decade having been released again in 1989.

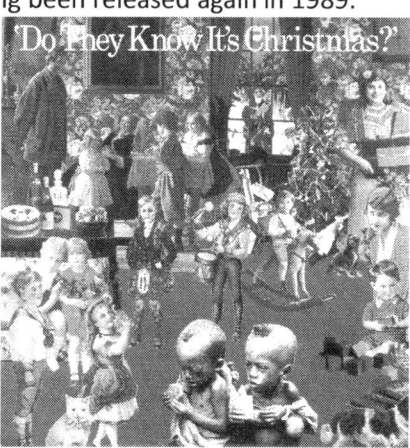

A less well-known charity, 'Ferry Aid', recorded the Beatles' song, **Let It Be** in 1987. This followed the sinking of the ferry 'Ms Herald of the Free' at Zeebrugge, killing 193 passengers and crew. The recording was organised by The Sun newspaper, after it had sold cheap tickets for the ferry on that day.

Tears For Fears, Duran Duran and Simple Minds got together and released **Everybody Wants to Rule the World** in 1986 in support of 'Sport Aid', a campaign to help tackle famine in Africa.

In 1983, Michael Jackson redefined the style, course, and possibilities of music videos. He released **Thriller** and made recording history. The album spent thirty-seven weeks at No 1 on the US Billboard chart. By early 1984, thirty million copies had been sold, and it was still selling at a rate of more than a million copies a week worldwide.

SCIENCE AND NATURE

The Compact Disc

In 1981, Kieran Prendiville on BBC's 'Tomorrow's World', demonstrated the CD and wondered, "Whether or not there is a market for these discs, remains to be seen." Well, on the 25th anniversary of its first public release in 1982, it was estimated that 200 billion CDs had been sold worldwide so I guess the answer was "Yes"!

At the end of the 70's, Philips and Sony had teamed up to begin working on CDs for the public and decided on a thin, shiny and circular storage disc, which could hold about 80 minutes of music. The disc had a diameter of 120mm, Sony having insisted that the longest musical performance, Beethoven's entire 9th Symphony at 74 minutes, should fit. A CD could hold an immense amount of data, much more than the vinyl record or the cassette and was perfectly portable.

The first commercial CD to be pressed was **Visitors** by Abba, followed quickly by the first album, Billy Joel's **52nd Street**. The biggest selling CD of all time is the Eagles 1976 **Their Greatest Hits** album, which has sold over 38 million copies.

UFOs in the Forest

On 26 December 1980, several US Airforce personnel stationed near the east gate at RAF Woodbridge, reported they had seen "lights" apparently descending into nearby Rendlesham Forest. They initially thought it was a downed aircraft but, upon investigation, they saw what they described as a glowing object, metallic in appearance, with coloured lights.

After daybreak on the morning of December 27, servicemen returned to a small clearing in the forest and found three small impressions on the ground in a triangular pattern, as well as burn marks and broken branches on nearby trees.

The 'Rendlesham Forest Incident' made headline news and theories suggest it was either an actual alien visitation, a secret military aircraft, a misinterpretation of natural lights, the beam of Orfordness Lighthouse, or just a hoax.

Mount St Helens

In March 1980 a series of volcanic explosions began at Mount St Helens, Washington in the US, culminating in a major explosive eruption on May 18. The eruption column rose 80,000 feet (15 miles) into the atmosphere and deposited ash over 11 states and into some Canadian provinces. At the same time, snow, ice, and entire glaciers on the volcano melted, forming a series of large volcanic mudslides that reached as far as 50 miles to the southwest. Thermal energy released during the eruption was equal to 26 megatons of TNT.

Regarded as the most significant and disastrous volcanic eruption in the country's history, about 57 people were killed, hundreds of square miles were reduced to wasteland, thousands of animals were killed, and Mount St. Helens was left with a crater on its north side. The area is now preserved as the Mount St Helens National Volcanic Monument.

One day before the eruption and several months afterwards. About a third of the mountain was blown away.

SPORT

1980 - 1984

1980 Eight days after the **Boston marathon**, Rosie Ruiz, a Cuban American, is disqualified as the winner 'in the fastest time ever run by a woman'. Investigations found that she did not run the entire course, joining about a half-mile before the finish.

Larry Holmes defeats Muhammed Ali to retain boxing's **WBC World Heavyweight** title. It is Ali's last world title bout.

1981 At **Wimbledon**, John McEnroe defeats Björn Borg to gain his 3rd career Grand Slam title and his 1st Wimbledon title.

In the ladies' final, Chris Evert Lloyd defeats Hana Mandlíková to gain her 12th career Grand Slam title and her third and last Wimbledon title.

1982 In June, at Pebble Beach, the American Tom Watson wins **The US Open** and a month later, at Royal Troon, he wins the **The Open.** He is only the third golfer, at that time, to win both Championships in the same year.

In Spain, Italy defeat West Germany in the **World Cup Final.** The tournament features the first penalty shoot-out in the World Cup competition.

1983 The **FA Cup** is won by Manchester United who, having drawn the first final with Brighton and Hove Albion, win the replay, 4-0.

1984 John McEnroe has his best season. He wins 13 singles tournaments, including **Wimbledon** where he loses just one set on his way to his third Wimbledon singles title. This includes a straight set win over Jimmy Connors in the final. He also wins the **US Open**, capturing the year-end number one ranking.

1985 - 1989

1985 Ireland is the championship winner in the **Rugby Five Nations** winning their tenth solo title, but it would prove to be their last for 24 years, until their Grand Slam in 2009.

Alain Prost becomes the **F1 World Champion** Driver, winning five of the sixteen Grand Prix. The first ever world championship **Australian Grand Prix** is held on a street circuit in Adelaide.

1986 In the **World Cup**, Argentina wins by defeating West Germany 3-2. Diego Maradona is the biggest star of the event, and his 'Hand of God' goal is well remembered. The event also sees the introduction of the 'Mexican Wave'.

1987 In **Cricket** the Indian opening batsman, Sunil Gavaskar reaches 10,000 test runs to become the first ever player to score this many. In the **Cricket World Cup** played for the first time outside Britain, in India, Australia win by defeating their arch-rivals, England.

1988 The **FA Cup** is won by Wimbledon FC's 'Crazy Gang', who defeat league champions Liverpool through a headed goal by Lawrie Sanchez. This is Wimbledon's only FA Cup title during its lifetime.

1989 On heavy, almost un-raceable ground, the iconic grey Desert Orchid, ridden by Simon Sherwood, in a race that defined his illustrious career, wins the **Cheltenham Gold Cup**. In 2005 this was voted the 'Greatest Race of All Time' by Racing Post readers.

You cannot be serious!

During the 1981 Wimbledon Championships, John McEnroe uttered what has become the most immortal phrase in tennis, if not all sport, when he screamed "you cannot be serious" at a Wimbledon umpire while disputing a line call. Already called "Superbrat" by the British tabloid press for his verbal volleys during previous Wimbledon matches, it was in a first-round match against fellow American Tom Gullikson, who was serving at 15-30 and 1-1 in the first set when a McEnroe shot was called out. Approaching the umpire, he said: "Chalk came up all over the place, you can't be serious man." Then, his anger rising, he bawled the words that would stay with him for a lifetime and find its way into the sporting annals. "You cannot be serious," he screamed. "That ball was on the line".

On the receiving end of the tirade was umpire Edward James, who eventually responded by politely announcing: "I'm going to award a point against you Mr McEnroe." It made little difference, McEnroe went on to win in straight sets and two weeks later had his final victory over Bjorn Borg.

Torvill and Dean

On Valentine's Day 1984, Jayne Torvill and Christopher Dean made history at the Winter Olympics in Sarajevo and set a new standard for world class figure skating. The duo from Nottingham, were the last to perform in their category and their performance, self-choreographed to 4½ minutes of Ravel's Bolero, was seamless, elegant and hypnotic. As they sank to the ice in the dramatic finale, the whole stadium stood and applauded. Their dance had captured the world's imagination and won Gold. The unanimous scores of 6.0 for artistic impression made them the highest-scoring figure skaters of all time.

Their routine, made Ravel's Boléro with its steady crescendo and repeated snare-drum rhythms, synonymous with figure-skating.

TRANSPORT

British Car Manufacturing

Gallery:

The 1980s was still a busy period for British car manufacturers and many of the bestselling cars of the decade were made in Britain.

The top 10 cars were:

1. Ford Escort
2. Vauxhall Cavalier
3. Ford Fiesta
4. Austin Metro
5. Ford Sierra (which replaced the
6. Ford Cortina)
6. Vauxhall Astra
7. Ford Orion
8. Austin Maestro
9. Vauxhall Nova
10. Ford Grenada

However the list of the **'Most influential Cars of the 1980s'** shows how the British car industry was soon to be decimated. The list includes:

Audi Quatrro; Porsche 944: Renault Scenic; Mercedes 190; BMW 3 Series; VW Golf; Volvo 240 Estate; Peugeot 205 and the Toyota Carolla.

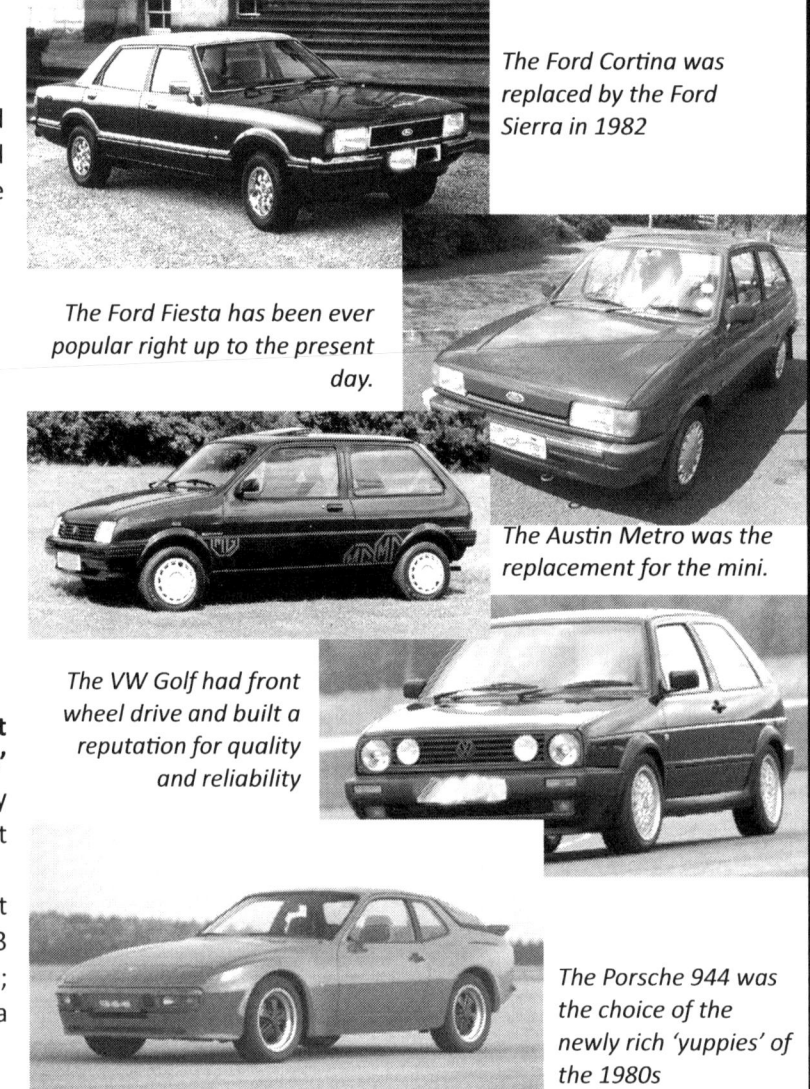

The Ford Cortina was replaced by the Ford Sierra in 1982

The Ford Fiesta has been ever popular right up to the present day.

The Austin Metro was the replacement for the mini.

The VW Golf had front wheel drive and built a reputation for quality and reliability

The Porsche 944 was the choice of the newly rich 'yuppies' of the 1980s

Clunk Click Every Trip

Although car manufacturers had been obliged to install seatbelts since 1965, it was not until January 1983 that the law requiring all drivers to wear their belts came into force. In spite of a great deal of 'grumbling' and more, ranging from *"the erosion of our civil liberties, another example of the Nanny State"*, to *"its uncomfortable, restrictive and creases my clothes"* and horror stories of crash victims being *"hanged"* by their belts or suffering greater injury, 90% of drivers and front seat passengers were observed to be wearing seat belts soon after the law came into effect – and these rates have been sustained since then. There was an immediate 25% reduction in driver fatalities and a 29 per cent reduction in fatal injuries among front seat passengers.

In 1989 it became compulsory for all children under 14 to wear a seat belt in the rear and when seatbelt wearing became compulsory for all rear-seat occupants in 1991, there was an immediate increase from 10% to 40% in observed seat belt wearing rates.

Aviation

When Airbus designed the A300 during the late 1960s and early 1970s, it envisaged a broad family of airliners with which to compete against Boeing and Douglas, the two established US aerospace manufacturers.

The launch of the A320 in 1987 guaranteed the status of Airbus as a major player in the aircraft market – the aircraft had over 400 orders before it first flew.

Motorcycles

Only 3000 Honda FVR750R motorcycles were made, race bred machines with lights thrown on to make them road legal and sold to the public. The first batch of 1000 sold out instantly. With a top speed of 153mph the V-four powered RC30 was one of the fastest sports bike of the decade but it was the track proven frame that meant it handled like a genuine racer. It also had a soundtrack to die for and was absolutely beautiful.

The Docklands Light Railway

The Docklands Light Railway was first opened in August 1987 as an automated, light metro system to serve the redeveloped Docklands area of London as a cheap public transport solution. The original network comprised two routes - Tower Gateway to Island Gardens and Stratford to Island Gardens and was mainly elevated on disused railway viaducts, new concrete viaducts and disused surface railway tracks. The trains were fully automated, controlled by computer, and had no driver.

They did however have a "Train Captain" who was responsible for patrolling the train, checking tickets, making announcements and controlling the doors. They could take control of the train should there be an equipment failure or emergency. The first generation of rolling stock comprised eleven lightweight units and the stations, mostly of a common design, constructed from standard components and usually featuring a short half-cylindrical, glazed, blue canopy, were designed specifically for these single articulated trains. The 15 stations were all above ground and needed no staff.

1990 - 1994

1990:
Feb: Nelson Mandela is released from prison in South Africa, after 27 years behind bars.

Nov: Margaret Thatcher resigns as Prime Minister. At 11 years, she was the longest serving PM of the 20th Century.

1991:
Jan: The Gulf War begins, as the Royal Air Force joins Allied aircraft in bombing raids on Iraq

Apr: After a year of protests and riots, the government confirms that the Poll Tax is to be replaced by a new Council Tax in 1993.

1992:
Apr: At the General Election the Conservative Party are re-elected for a fourth term under John Major.

Nov: Part of Windsor Castle is gutted in a fire causing millions of pounds worth of damage and The Queen describes this year as an Annus Horribilis.

1993:
Apr: The Queen announces that Buckingham Palace will open to the public for the first time

Sep: The UK Independence Party which supports the breakaway from the EU is formed.

Dec: Diana, Princess of Wales. withdraws from public life.

1994:
Mar: The Church of England ordains its first female priests.

May: The Channel Tunnel between Britain and France is officially opened.

Nov: The first UK National Lottery draw takes place.

1992: The 'Maastricht Treaty' was concluded between the 'then' twelve member states of the European Communities. This foundation treaty of the EU announced a new stage in the process of European integration, shared citizenship and a single currency. There were two headquarters, one in Brussels and one in Strasbourg,

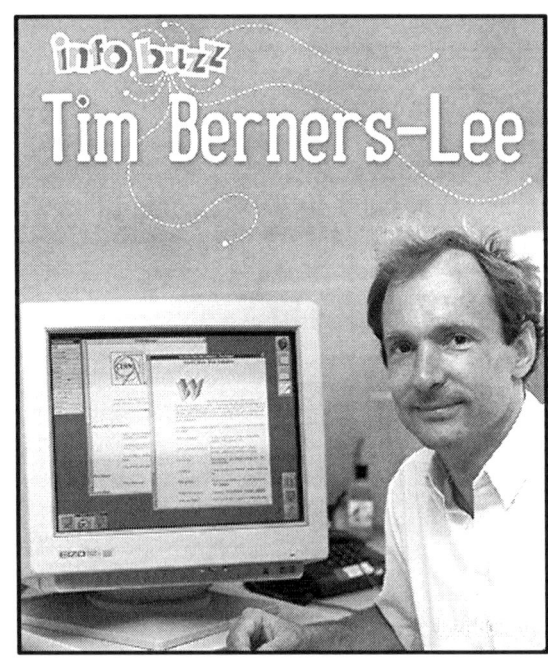

1991: The internet already existed but no one had thought of a way of how to link one document directly to another until in 1989, British scientist Tim Berners-Lee, invented the WorldWideWeb. The www. was introduced in 1991 as the first web browser and the first website went online in August.

1995 - 1999

1997: The UK transfers sovereignty of Hong Kong, the largest remaining British colony, to the People's Republic of China as the 99 years lease on the territory formally ends.

1999: On 1ˢᵗ January, the new European currency, the Euro is launched and some 320 million people from eleven European countries begin carrying the same money in their wallets.
Britain's Labour government preferred to stay with the pound sterling instead.

1995:
Feb: Barings Bank, the UK's oldest merchant bank, collapses after rogue trader Nick Leeson loses $1.4 billion.

Apr: All telephone area dialling codes are changed in the UK.

Aug: Pubs in England are permitted to remain open throughout Sunday afternoon.

1996:
Feb: The Prince and Princess of Wales agree to divorce more than three years after separating.

Jul: Dolly the Sheep becomes the first mammal to be successfully cloned from an adult cell.

1997:
May: Tony Blair wins a landslide General Election for the Labour Party.

Aug: Princess Diana is killed in a car crash in Paris. Dodi Fayed, the heir to the Harrods empire is killed with her

1998:
Mar: Construction on the Millenium Dome begins. It will be the centre piece for a national celebration.

Apr: The Good Friday Agreement between the UK and Irish governments is signed.

1999:
Apr: A minimum wage is introduced in the UK – set at £3.60 an hour for workers over 21, and £3 for workers under 21

Jun: Construction of the Millenium Dome is finished and in October, the London Eye begins to be lifted into position.

THE HOME

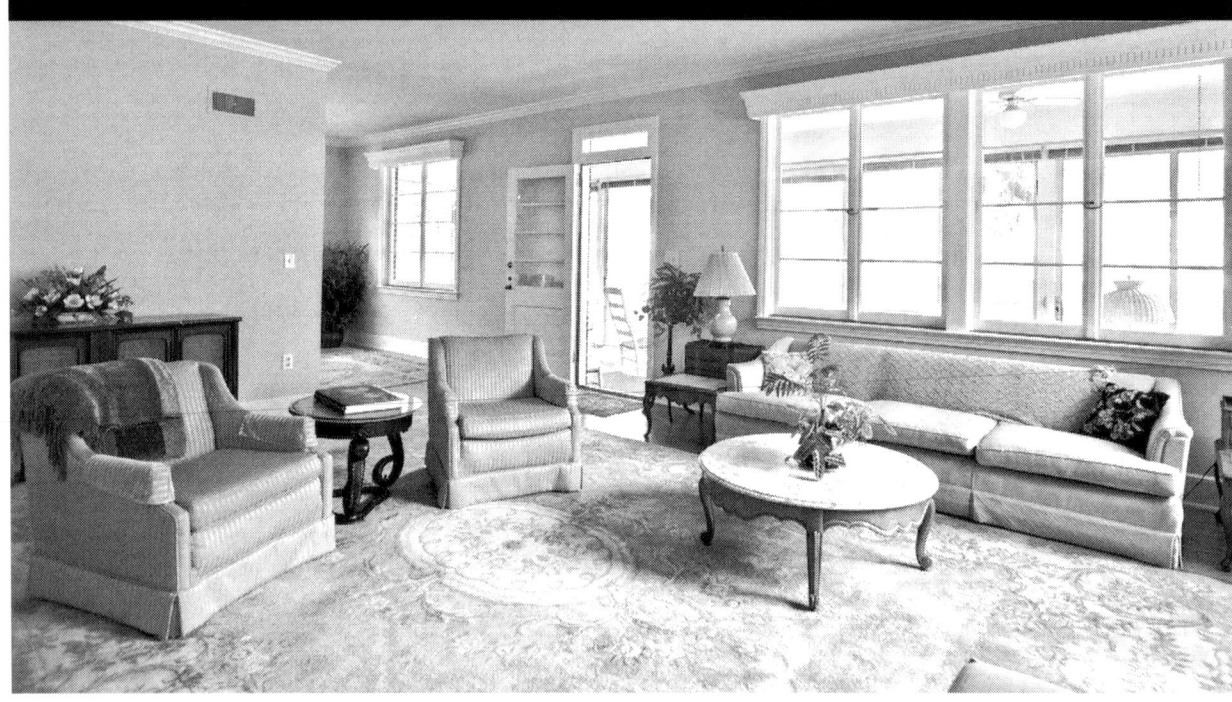

Home life in the 1990s was changing again. Family time was not cherished as it had once been, children had a lot more choice and were becoming more independent with their own TVs programmes, personal computers, music systems, mobile phones and, crucially, the introduction of the world wide web, which meant life would never be the same again.

After school and weekend organised activities for the young burgeoned, with teenagers able to take advantage of the fast-food chains, or eating at different times, meaning no more family eating together. Families 'lived in separate' rooms, there were often two televisions so different channels could be watched and children wanted to play with their Nintendos or listen to their Walkmans in their own rooms. Their rooms were increasingly themed, from Toy Story to Athena posters, a ceiling full of sticker stars that illuminated a room with their green glow and somewhere in the house, room had to be made for the computer desk.

Track lighting was an easy way to illuminate a room without relying on multiple lamps and it became a popular feature in many '90s homes along with corner baths — most of which also had a water jet function which suddenly turned your bath into a low-budget jacuzzi!

In 1990, 68% of UK households owned at least one car, and the use of 'out of town' supermarkets and shopping centres, where just about anything and everything could be purchased in the same area, meant that large weekly or even monthly shops could be done in a single outing and combined with the huge increase in domestic freezers and ready prepared foods, time spent in the kitchen and cooking could be greatly reduced.

Over 80% of households owned a washing machine and 50%, a tumble dryer, so the need to visit the laundrette all but disappeared and instead of "Monday is washing day", the family's laundry could be carried out on an 'as and when' basis. All contributing to an increase in leisure time.

Nearly three-quarters of homes had microwave cookers and for working women who did not want to do their own cleaning, Merry Maids set up their home cleaning franchise in the UK in 1990 and many other companies followed suit.

Commuting

In Great Britain at the beginning of the 1990s, the *average* one-way commute to work was 38 minutes in London, 33 minutes in the south-east, and 21 minutes in the rest of the country. By the end of the decade, full-time workers commuting to and from London, had lost an additional 70 minutes per week of home time to commuting but, by contrast, outside the south-east of Britain, there was no increase in commuting time over the decade. In the south-east, 30% of workers took at least 45 minutes to get to work. In the rest of the country, only 10% did.

ART AND CULTURE

1990 - 1994

1990 In Rome, on the eve of the final of the FIFA World Cup, the Three Tenors sing together for the first time. The event is broadcast live and watched worldwide by millions of people. The highlight is Luciano Pavarotti's performance of Nessun Dorma.
The first Hampton Court Palace Flower Show takes place.

1991 Dame Margot Fonteyn, the Royal Ballet's Prima Ballerina, dies in Panama City, exactly 29 years after her premiere with Rudolf Nureyev who made his debut in 'Giselle'.

1992 Damien Hirst's "Shark", featuring a preserved shark, is first shown at an exhibition at the Saatchi Gallery in London.
Under the new Further and Higher Education Act, Polytechnics are allowed to become new Universities and award degrees of their own.
The last edition of Punch, the UK's oldest satirical magazine since 1841, is published.

1993 Bookmakers cut their odds on the monarchy being abolished by the year 2000 from 100 to 1 to 50 to 1.
QVC launches the first television shopping channel in the UK.

1994 The Duchess of Kent joins the Roman Catholic Church, the first member of the Royal Family to convert to Catholicism for more than 300 years.
The Sunday Trading Act comes into full effect, permitting retailers to trade on Sundays but restricts larger stores to a maximum of six hours, between 10 am and 6 pm.

1995 - 1999

1995 The first ever World Book Day was held on 23rd April, picked to celebrate the anniversary of William Shakespeare's death.

The BBC begins regular Digital Audio Broadcasting from Crystal Palace.

1996 Shortly after publication of the Italian edition of his book 'The Art Forger's Handbook', English-born art forger, Eric Hebborn is beaten to death in Rome.
The Stone of Scone is installed in Edinburgh Castle 700 years after it was removed from Scotland by King Edward I of England.

1997 The Teletubbies caused a sensation when they appeared on BBC TV. They were the most sought-after toy of the year.
The reconstruction of the Elizabethan Globe Theatre, called Shakespeare's Globe opens in London with a production of Shakespeare's 'Henry V'.

1998 Britain's largest sculpture, the Angel of the North by Anthony Gormley is installed at Low Eighton, Gateshead.
More than 15,000 people attend a tribute concert held for Diana, Princess of Wales, at her family home, Althorp Park.

1999 The children's picture book, 'The Gruffalo' by Julia Donaldson is first published.

Media coverage for the Turner Prize was dominated by extreme critical response to Tracey Emin's work 'My Bed' – an installation of her unmade bed, complete with dirty sheets and detritus.

1997: 'Harry Potter and the Philosopher's Stone' by JK Rowling made its debut in June. The initial edition of this first book in the series, comprised 500 copies and the novel has gone on to sell in excess of 120 million. The success of the whole Harry Potter phenomenon is well known, and there have been less expected benefits too. Certainly, before the films, children loved reading the books and boosted the reported numbers of children reading and indeed, reading longer books.

The perception of boarding schools, often associated with misery and cruel, spartan regimes was changed for some by Hogwarts School of Witchcraft and Wizardry. The sense of excitement, community and friendship of the children, the camaraderie of eating together and playing together, made going away to school more appealing for many.

The amazing visual effects used in the films were instrumental in persuading Hollywood to consider UK technical studios and raised the number of visual effects Oscar nominations for British companies significantly.

1997: The Guggenheim Museum of modern and contemporary art, designed by Canadian-American architect Frank Gehry, opened in Bilbao. The building represents an architectural landmark of innovating design, a spectacular structure.

The museum was originally a controversial project. Bilbao's industry, steel and shipbuilding was dying, and the city decided to regenerate to become a modern technological hub of the Basque region, and the controversy was, instead of an office block or factory, the centre piece would be a brand-new art gallery.

It is a spectacular building, more like a sculpture with twisted metal, glass, titanium and limestone, a futuristic setting for fine works of art. The gamble paid off, in the first twenty years, the museum attracted more than 19 million visitors with 70% from outside Spain. Foreign tourists continue to travel through the Basque country bringing a great economic boost to the region and Bilbao itself, has transformed from a grimy post-industrial town to a tourist hotspot.

FILMS

1990 - 1994

1990 It was Oscar time for an epic western this year and **Dances With Wolves**, directed and starring Kevin Costner with seven Academy Awards, won Best Picture and Best Director. It is one of only three Westerns to win the Oscar for Best Picture, the other two being **Cimmaron** in 1931 and **Unforgotten** in **1992**.

1991 *"Well, Clarice - have the lambs stopped screaming?"* wrote Dr Hannibal Lecter to the young FBI trainee, Clarice Starling. The thriller, **The Silence of the Lambs**, about a cannibalistic serial killer, scared audiences half to death and won the Best Picture Award.

1992 The nominations for the Academy Awards held some serious themes. **The Crying Game** was set against the backdrop of the 'troubles' in Northern Ireland. There was a blind retired Army officer in **Scent of a Woman**, rising troubles in colonial French Vietnam in **Indochine** and the invasion of Panama in **The Panama Deception**.

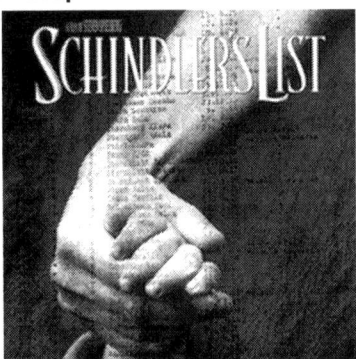

1993 The acclaimed **Schindler's List** won Best Picture with stiff competition from **The Piano** which won Best Original Screenplay and Robin Williams as **Mrs Doubtfire** which became the second highest grossing film of the year.

1994 Disney's animated musical **The Lion King** made the most money this year, but **Forest Gump** took the prize for Best Picture. The British film **Four Weddings and a Funeral** was a huge success and brought WH Auden's beautiful poem 'Funeral Blues' into the limelight.

1995 - 1999

1995 The tense, amazingly technically correct, story of the ill-fated **Apollo 13** quest to land on the moon failed to win the top Oscar, beaten by Mel Gibson in **Braveheart**, the American take on the story of William Wallace and the first Scottish war of independence against England.

1996 The English Patient a romantic war drama won the Best Picture, up against Mike Leigh's **Secrets and Lies** which won the Best British Film.

1997 The blockbuster **Titanic** was the film of the year. The combination of romance and disaster proving irresistible. Harland & Wolfe, the builders of RMS Titanic shared blueprints they thought were lost with the crew to produce the scale models, computer-generated imagery and a reconstruction of the ship itself, to re-create the sinking.

1998 Shakespeare in Love, a fictional love affair between Shakespeare and Viola de Lesseps whilst he is writing Romeo and Juliet was hugely popular and won seven Oscars.

1999 In **American Beauty,** Kevin Spacey plays Lester Burnham, an unhappy executive whose midlife awakening is the crux of the story. Bad as he thinks his life is, he cannot not stop seeing the beauty of the world around him.

**"Fear can hold you prisoner,
Hope can set you free."**

In 1994, Tim Robbins and Morgan Freeman starred **The Shawshank Redemption**, an inspirational, life-affirming and uplifting, old-fashioned style prison film and character study in the ilk of 'The Birdman of Alcatraz'. Set in a fictional, oppressive Shawshank State Prison in Maine, two imprisoned men bond over the years, in a tale of friendship, patience, hope, survival and ultimately finding solace and eventual redemption through acts of common decency.

The film was initially a box office disappointment. Many reasons were put forward for its failure at the time, including a general unpopularity of prison films, its lack of female characters and even the title, which was considered to be confusing. However, it was nominated for seven Academy Awards, failed to win a single Oscar, but this raised awareness and increased the film's popularity such that it is now preserved in the US National Film Registry as "culturally, historically, or aesthetically significant".

The Full Monty

In 1997 whilst huge audiences were crying over Kate Winslet and Leonardo di Caprio in **Titanic,** equally huge audiences were laughing at the story of six unemployed men in Sheffield, four of them former steel workers, who are in dire need of cash and who decide to emulate 'The Chippendales' dance, striptease troupe. They devise a dance act with their difference being, that Gaz decides their show must be even better than the originals and declares to the friends that they will go 'the full

Monty' – they will strip all the way. Although primarily a comedy, the film touches on several serious subjects too, including unemployment, father's rights – Gaz is unable to pay maintenance to his estranged wife and she is seeking sole custody of his son – and working-class culture, depression and suicide. The film was a huge success as it ultimately is about humanity and the problems people all over the world struggle with.

Fashion

Supermodels

The original supermodels of the 1980s, Linda Evangelista, Naomi Campbell, Christy Turlington and Cindy Crawford were joined later by Claudia Schiffer and then Kate Moss to become the "Big Six". Models used to be categorised as 'print' or 'runway' but the "Big Six" showed that they could do it all, catwalk, print campaigns, magazine covers and even music videos and they became pop 'icons' in their own right. The models were also known for their earning capacity, one famous remark from Linda Evangelista, "We don't wake up for less than $10,000 a day!"

But with the popularity of grunge, came a shift away from the fashion for feminine curves and wholesome looking women, and in came the rise of a new breed of fragile, individual-looking and often younger, models, epitomised by Kate Moss. Her waif-like thinness and delicacy complemented the unkempt look that was popular in the early nineties and a new phrase 'heroin chic' described the down-at-heel settings for fashion shoots presented in magazines. By the end of the decade however, attitudes had shifted and concern about the health of the skeletal model was becoming a source of great debate.

Goth

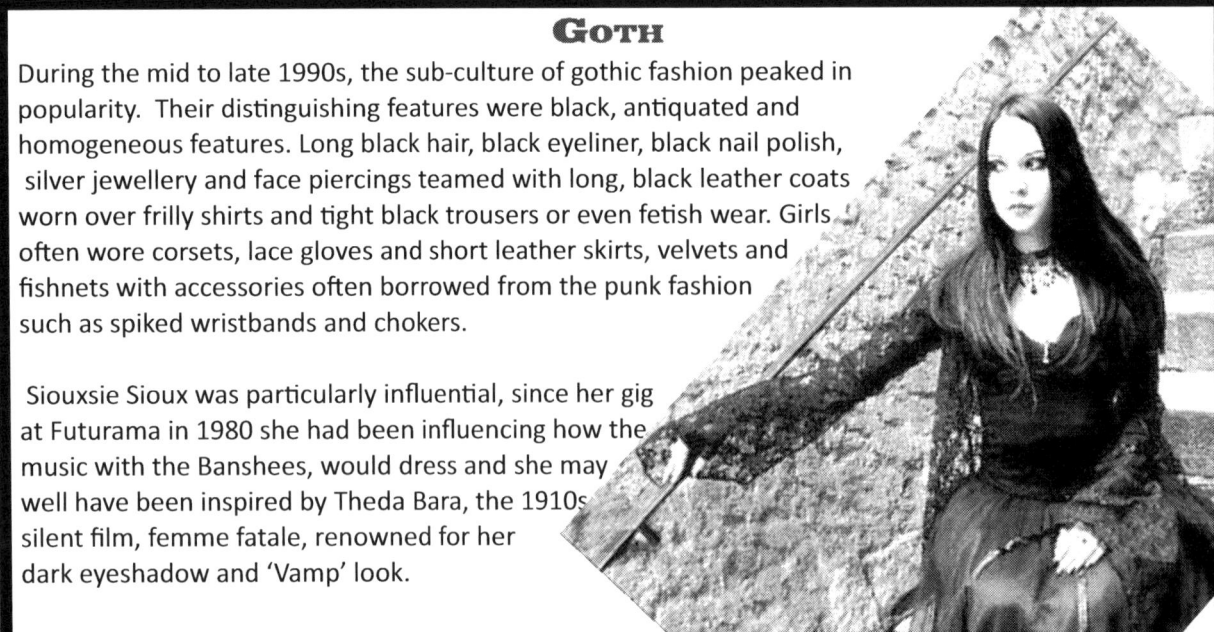

During the mid to late 1990s, the sub-culture of gothic fashion peaked in popularity. Their distinguishing features were black, antiquated and homogeneous features. Long black hair, black eyeliner, black nail polish, silver jewellery and face piercings teamed with long, black leather coats worn over frilly shirts and tight black trousers or even fetish wear. Girls often wore corsets, lace gloves and short leather skirts, velvets and fishnets with accessories often borrowed from the punk fashion such as spiked wristbands and chokers.

Siouxsie Sioux was particularly influential, since her gig at Futurama in 1980 she had been influencing how the music with the Banshees, would dress and she may well have been inspired by Theda Bara, the 1910s silent film, femme fatale, renowned for her dark eyeshadow and 'Vamp' look.

In The 1990s

Grunge

Grunge was a style for the young that emerged in Seattle in the late 1980s and by the early 90s had spread across the world. Made popular by bands such as Nirvana, it was a fashion for both men and women. The look was simple, an oversized flannel shirt, sometimes worn over a t-shirt, and baggy, worn out jeans to give an overall, dishevelled, appearance. The clothes were found ideally in charity shops or at the back of "Dad's wardrobe". A pair of Doc Martens or Converse shoes finished the ensemble.

Nirvana's lead singer Kurt Cobain epitomised the look with holes in his jeans and cardigan sweaters and the fashion world caught on when their second album, 'Nevermind' was released in 1991 and grunge made it onto the catwalk – specifically by Calvin Klein on an 18-year-old Kate Moss. Shrunken baby doll dresses, old prom dresses or even old petticoats and simple slip dresses appeared, often worn with chunky boots and for men, beanies, band t-shirts and knitted sweaters with patterns.

Friends

For women, long loose hair was the most popular women's style, but the most requested hairstyle of the 1990s was said to be 'The Rachel'. Jennifer Anniston's character in 'Friends', Rachel Green, had the haircut people wanted – bouncy, layered, shoulder length, obviously styled to within an inch of its life yet at the same time artfully tousled.

Hoodies

Utilitarian styles such as cargo pants and The Gap's hooded sweatshirts became popular for everyday wear. Industrial and military styles crept into mainstream fashion and camouflage pants were everywhere on the street.
There was also a concerted move towards logoed clothing such as by Tommy Hilfiger

LEISURE

THE GAMES CHILDREN PLAYED

The trend in the 90s was for more electronic, video and computer games but younger children still enjoyed many of the traditional past-times, and events in the 90s such as the FIFA World Cups and the Olympics, produced special collections which reignited interest in collecting 'stickers,' and filling albums.

Crazes were still all the craze too and it was digital pets like Tamagotchi, housed in their small, egg-shaped, handheld video game console that became the biggest fads of the end of the decade.

The Teletubbies caused a huge sensation in 1997, communicating through gibberish and designed to resemble real-life toddlers, they became a huge commercial success, the toy Teletubbies being the most demanded toy of 1997.

However, it was Sony's PlayStation which was the big innovation of the 90s. The first version was able to process games stored on CD-ROMs and introduced 3D graphics to the industry. It had a low retail price and Sony employed aggressive youth marketing. Ridge Racer was the classic motor racing game used in the launch and the popularity of this game was crucial to the early success of the PlayStation.

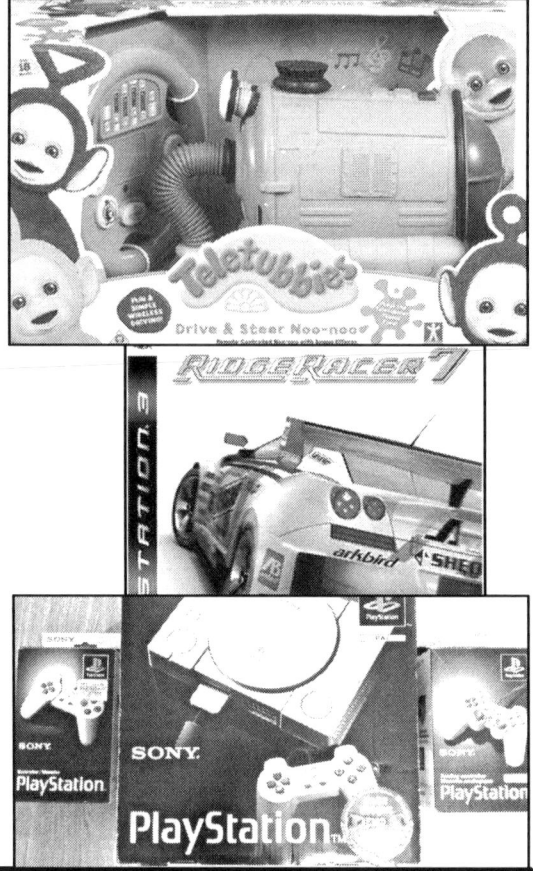

RESTORATION OF THE SPA

From being at the centre of society in previous times, the spa industry had declined so much that by the 50s, leading spas such as those at Buxton, Cheltenham and Tunbridge Wells had closed. The 1990s saw a simultaneous rise of increasing disposable wealth, and the popularity of a new concept of the spa, pure self-indulgence and pampering.

The need to pause and detox from time to time fitted nicely into the growth of a 'wellness' culture and the understanding of holistic wellbeing, treatments to soothe the mind, body and spirit. Wearing a luxurious white robe and slippers, lounging by a heated pool reading magazines and dipping from time to time into the whirlpools, a trip to the steam room or sauna before taking a light lunch and then unwinding to a fragranced oil body massage because, as L'Oreal had been saying since the 70s, "you're worth it!"

Where We Went on Holiday

In the 90s, if we went on a foreign holiday at all, 26m of us in 1996, the norm was to go for just the one, two-week summer break. Booking with a Travel Agent in town or finding a cheap package deal on Teletext, we arrived at our destination with a guide-book, Travellers Cheques and a camera complete with film.

Our favourite places were Spain and France, many of us travelling on the cross-Channel ferries rather than on the budget airlines. Our other favourite hot spots were Belgium, Turkey, Egypt, Kenya and Tunisia.

Although the gap year began in the 1960s, it was in the 1990s when the idea became the 'thing to do' amongst the children of the new wealthy middle classes.

Many visited India, Pakistan and Nepal, Australia, Thailand, the USA and New Zealand being their favoured countries to visit.

Some did voluntary work in the developing nations, building schools and teaching children English.

The 90s saw plenty of new cruise ships being launched for what became a massive growth industry. New cruise lines were formed, and many existing lines merged and Royal Caribbean, Celebrity, Fred Olsen and Carnival, Disney, Silver Sea and Princess lines were all introducing, predominantly older people, to new places and entertaining them royally on the way.

For others, at the opposite end of the cruising scale, was the immensely popular, 'Booze Cruise'. The day trip across the channel to France to stock up on duty free wine and cigarettes.

MUSIC

1990 - 1994

1990 Elton John's **Sacrifice** was initially released as a single in 1989 but only reached No. 55 in the UK. In mid-1990, Radio 1 DJ, Steve Wright began playing it and it soon caught on with other DJs and when re-released as a double A-side single with **Healing Hands** it became John's first solo No 1 single remaining at the top for five weeks.

1991 Cher made the 1960s **Shoop Shoop Song (It's in His Kiss)** an international hit once again. **(Everything I Do) I Do It for You**, from the soundtrack of the film 'Robin Hood: Prince of Thieves' was sung by Bryan Adams and became a huge hit, the best-selling single of the year and stayed at No 1 for 16 weeks.

1992 Shakespeares Sister had their only No 1 UK single hit with **Stay** which stayed at the top for eight consecutive weeks.
The best-selling single of the year was Whitney Houston singing the song written by Dolly Parton, **I Will Always Love You.**

1993 Pray by Take That, written by Gary Barlow, was the first of twelve singles by the band to reach No 1 in the UK and the first of a run of four consecutive No 1's.

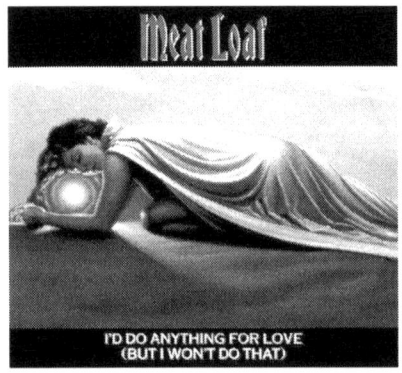

I'd Do Anything for Love (But I Won't Do That) was the song of the year and won Meat Loaf a Grammy Award for the Best Rock Solo Vocal Performance.

1994 The Most Beautiful Girl in the World by the unpronounceable Love Symbol, or 'The Artist Formerly Known as Prince' reached No 1.
The Manchester United football squad had the help of Status Quo, who wrote and sang along on their two week No 1 hit, **Come on You Reds.**

1995 - 1999

1995 Four artists had two No 1 hits this year. The Outhere Brothers with **Don't Stop (Wiggle Wiggle)** and **Boom Boom Boom**. Take That with **Back for Good** and **Never Forget** and Robson Green & Jerome Flynn with **Unchained Melody/ Bluebirds Over the White Cliffs of Dover** – the best seller of the year, and **I Believe/Up On the Roof.**

1996 This was a year with 23 No 1s. Most being at the top for only one week, but Fugees was No 1 twice with the same song **Killing Me Softly.** Firstly, for four weeks in June and then with a break for a week for **Three Lions (Football's Coming Home)** and another week in July.

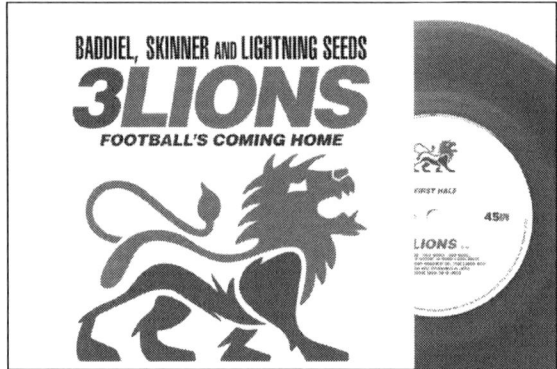

1997 Elton John topped the charts for five weeks with **Candle in the Wind 1997**, a re-written and re-recorded version of **Candle in the Wind** as a tribute to the late Diana, Princess of Wales.
Another kind of tribute, this time to the popularity of the Teletubbies, their **Teletubbies say 'Eh-oh!'** stayed at No 1 for two weeks in December.

1998 The main soundtrack song from the blockbuster film Titanic provided Celine Dion with a hit, **My Heart Will Go On.**
Cher reinvented herself, and her song, **Believe** stayed at No 1 for seven weeks and was the year's best seller.

1999 Britney Spears made her debut single with **...Baby One More Time** which became a worldwide hit and sold over ten million copies.
Cliff Richard's **Millenium Prayer** is knocked off its 3 weeks at No 1 spot just in time for the boy band, Westlife, to make the Christmas No 1 with **I Have a Dream/Seasons in the Sun.**

IN THE 1990s

COOL BRITANNIA

Throughout the mid and second half of the 1990s, Cool Britannia was a period of increased pride in the culture of the UK inspired by the 'Swinging London' of the 1960s pop culture. This brought about a huge success of 'Britpop' with groups such as Blur and Oasis and particularly, the Spice Girls.

Mel B, 'Scary Spice', Melanie C, 'Sporty Spice', Emma Bunton, 'Baby Spice', Geri Halliwell, 'Ginger Spice' and Victoria Beckham, 'Posh Spice' brought girl power to the fore. Their first single was 1996's iconic **Wannabe**, which established the group as a global phenomenon as 'Spice Mania' circled the globe. They scored the Christmas Number 1 single three years in a row and had nine UK No 1's in total.

LOVE IS ALL AROUND

In June 1994, Wet Wet Wet the Scottish soft rock band had a huge international hit, with 15 weeks as the UK No 1, with their cover of the 1960s hit by The Troggs, **Love Is All Around.** Their version was used on the soundtrack of the blockbuster film 'Four Weddings and a Funeral'.

Richard Curtis, the director of the film, had approached Wet Wet Wet with a choice of three cover songs to record for the soundtrack, the other two being **I Will Survive** by Gloria Gaynor and Barry Manilow's **Can't Smile Without You**.

SCIENCE AND NATURE

THE HUBBLE TELESCOPE

The Hubble telescope is a general-purpose orbiting observatory. Orbiting approximately 380 mi (612 km) above Earth, the 12.5-ton Hubble Space Telescope has peered farther into the universe than any telescope before it. The Hubble, which was launched on April 24, 1990, has produced images with unprecedented resolution at visible, near-ultraviolet, and near-infrared wavelengths since its originally faulty optics were corrected in 1993.

Although ground-based telescopes are finally starting to catch up, the Hubble continues to produce a stream of unique observations. During the 1990s and now into the 2000s, the Hubble has revolutionised the science of astronomy, becoming one, if not the most, important instruments ever used in astronomy.

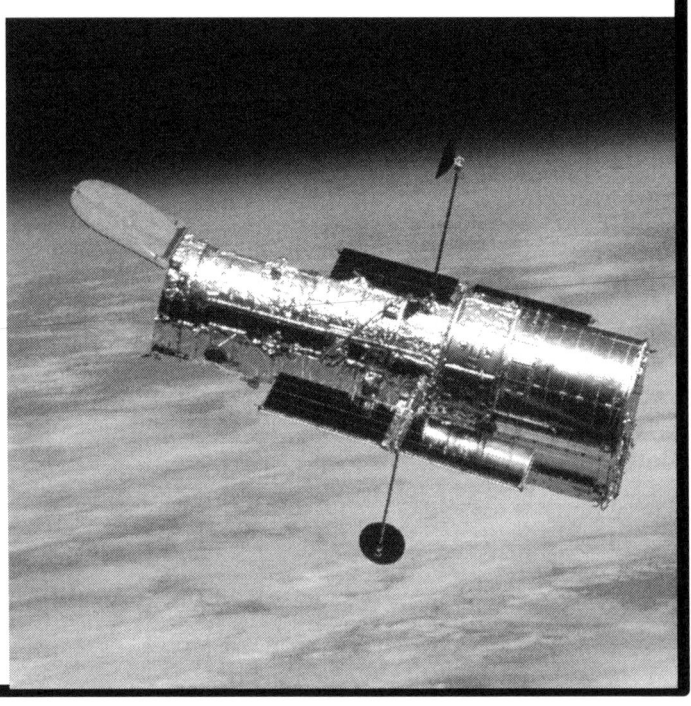

ADD TO BASKET

Mint Velvet Star Print Jumper, Pink

£69.00

Free Click & Collect over £30 & free returns
View delivery & returns options

Size.   size guide

XS   S   M   L

XL

Add to your basket

Add to wish list

ROYAL ALBERT OLD COUNTRY ROSES 40 PIECE DINNER TEA SET SERVICE TEASET ENGLAND

Condition: Used
Time left: 32m 7s | (31 Mar 2022 12:25:54 GMT)

Current   £185.00   [32 bids]
bid:
           Bid amount   Submit bid

Enter £190.00
or more   Watch this item

Posts from United Kingdom

The first ever shopper bought online from Tesco in 1984 using her television remote control, but it was in 1990s, following the creation by Tim Berners-Lee of the World Wide Web server and browser and the commercialisation of the internet in 1991 giving birth to e-commerce, that online shopping really began to take off.

In 1995, Amazon began selling books online, computer companies started using the internet for *all* their transactions and Auction Web was set up by Pierre Omidyar as a site *"dedicated to bringing together buyers and sellers in an honest and open marketplace."* We now know this as eBay and we can buy just about anything on Amazon.

Comparison sites were set up in 1997 and in 1998, PayPal was founded, the way to pay online without having to share your financial information. By 1999, online only shops were beginning to emerge and paved the way for 'Click for Checkout' to become commonplace.

In The 1990s

The Kyoto Protocol

In December 1997, at the instigation of the United Nations, representatives from 160 countries met in Kyoto, Japan, to discuss climate change and draft the Kyoto Protocol which aimed to restrict the greenhouse gas emissions associated with global warming.

The protocol focused on demands that 37 developed nations work to reduce their greenhouse gas emissions placing the burden on developed nations, viewing them as the primary sources and largely responsible for carbon emissions.

Developing nations were asked only to comply voluntarily, exempted from the protocol's requirements. The protocol's approach included establishing a 'carbon credits system' whereby nations can earn credits by participating in emission reduction projects in other nations. A carbon credit is a tradeable permit or certificate that provides the holder

Shock Waves

A large earthquake, by British standards, occurred near Bishop's Castle, Shropshire on the Welsh Borders on 2 April 1990 at 13:46 GMT. With a magnitude of 5.1, the shock waves were felt over a wide area of Britain, from Ayrshire in the north to Cornwall in the south, Kent in the east and Dublin in the west.

Worldwide in 1990, there were 18 quakes of magnitude 7.0 or above and 134 quakes between 6.0 and 7.0, 4435 quakes between 4.0 and 5.0, 2755 quakes between 3.0 and 4.0, and 8618 quakes between 2.0 and 3.0. There were also 29800 quakes below magnitude 2.0 which people don't normally feel.

The strongest quake was north of Pulau Hulawa Island in Indonesia, registering 7.8 on the Richter scale.

SPORT

1990 - 1994

1990 West Germany won the **FIFA World Cup** in Rome, defeating defending champions Argentina, 1–0 in the final.

The British golfer, Nick Faldo, had an amazing year, winning both the **Masters** and the Claret Jug at the **Open** at St Andrews, and capturing the PGA Player of the Year award, the first non-American to do so.

1991 At the **World Athletics** Championships in Tokyo, Mike Powell broke the 23 year-long world record **long jump** set by Bob Beamon, with a jump of 29' 4½".

1992 The rugby, **Five Nations Championship** is won by England who complete the Grand Slam for the second consecutive year.

The summer **Olympics** are held in Barcelona, Spain where Sally Gunnell takes home gold in the Women's 400 metres hurdles, Linford Christie triumphs in the Men's 100 metres, and rowers Matthew Pinsent and Steve Redgrave finish first in the Men's coxless pair, the first Olympic gold for all four athletes. In the **Paralympics**, Tanni Grey-Thompson in her debut Games, takes home four golds and a silver.

1993 Manchester United win the inaugural **English Premier League** title, their first league title in 26 years.

Shane Warne bowls the so-called 'Ball of the Century' in the first Test at Old Trafford. With his first ball against England, in his first **Ashes**, he bowled Mike Gatting out.

1994 Tiger Woods becomes the youngest man ever to win the **U.S. Amateur Golf Championships**, at age 18.

George Foreman becomes **Boxing's** oldest Heavyweight Champion at forty-five.

1995 - 1999

1995 In motor racing, Michael Schumacher wins his second consecutive **Drivers' Championship**, and Benetton wins its first and only Constructors' Championship.

British triple jumper Jonathan Edwards sets a world record in the **Athletics World Championships**, jumping 60' (18.29 m).

1996 The 95/96 **Rugby League** ends with Wigan declared champions.

Stephen Hendry wins the **World Snooker Championship** and remains the world number one.

1997 At 21, Tiger Woods becomes the youngest **Masters** winner in history, as well as the first non-white winner at Augusta. He set the scoring record at 270 and the record for the largest margin of victory at 12 strokes.

1998 In Japan, **Curling** is included in the Winter Olympics for the first time.

1999 Pete Sampras beats his biggest rival, Andre Agassi in the **Wimbledon Men's Singles** Final giving him his sixth win at the All England Club.

In the **US Open Tennis** final, at the age of 17, Serena Williams beats the number one player Martina Hingis and marks the beginning of one of the most dominant careers in the history of women's tennis.

THE DANGEROUS SIDE TO SPORT

By 1993, Monica Seles, the Serbian-American tennis player, had won eight Grand Slam titles and was ranked No. 1 in the world. On April 30, 1993, then just 19, she was sitting on a courtside seat during a changeover in a match in Hamburg when a German man, said later to be a fan of the tennis star's German rival, Steffi Graf, leaned over a fence and stabbed her between the shoulder blades with a knife. The assailant was quickly apprehended and Seles was taken to the hospital with a wound half and inch deep in her upper back. She recovered from her physical injuries but was left with deep emotional scars and didn't play again professionally for another two years.

Leading up to the 1994 Winter Olympics, figure skater Nancy Kerrigan was attacked during a practice session. This had been 'commissioned' by the ex-husband of fellow skater, Tonya Harding and her bodyguard. Kerrigan was Harding's long-time rival and the one person in the way of her making the Olympic team, and she was desperate to win. Fortunately for Kerrigan, the injury left her with just bruises – no broken bones but she had to withdraw from the U.S. Figure Skating Championship the following night. However, she was still given a spot on the Olympic team and finished with a silver medal. Harding finished in eighth place and later had her U.S. Figure Skating Championship title revoked and was banned from the United States Figure Skating Association for life.

Also in 1994, Andrés Escobar the Colombian footballer, nicknamed 'The Gentleman' - known for his clean style of play and calmness on the pitch - was murdered following a second-round match against the US in the FIFA World Cup. This was reportedly in retaliation for Escobar having scored an own goal which contributed to the team's elimination from the tournament.

In 1997, Evander Holyfield and Mike Tyson's fight made headlines after Tyson was disqualified for biting off a part of his rival's ear, an infamous incident that would lead to the event being dubbed "The Bite Fight".

TRANSPORT

HAULAGE

The 1990s was a decade devoted to environmental considerations for haulage with top priority given to cleaner emissions and low noise levels. By the end of the decade, integrated IT solutions were being used to provide the tools necessary to increase efficiency and safety.

A significant factor in the 1990s was making the lorry more aerodynamic. A 20% saving in fuel consumption meant lower emissions and also the average transport operator could improve profits by up to 50%.

CRUISE SHIPS

The largest passenger ship of the 1990s was Royal Caribbean's 'Voyager of the Seas' at 137,276 gross tonnage and 310 m (1,020 ft) long.

This record was held between Oct 1999 and Sep 2000, when it was superseded by 'Explorer of the Seas', larger by only 12 GT. Royal Caribbean have, on order, and due 2024, an Oasis class cruiser of 231,000 gross tonnage, 362 m(1,188 ft) long.

THE HIGHWAY CODE

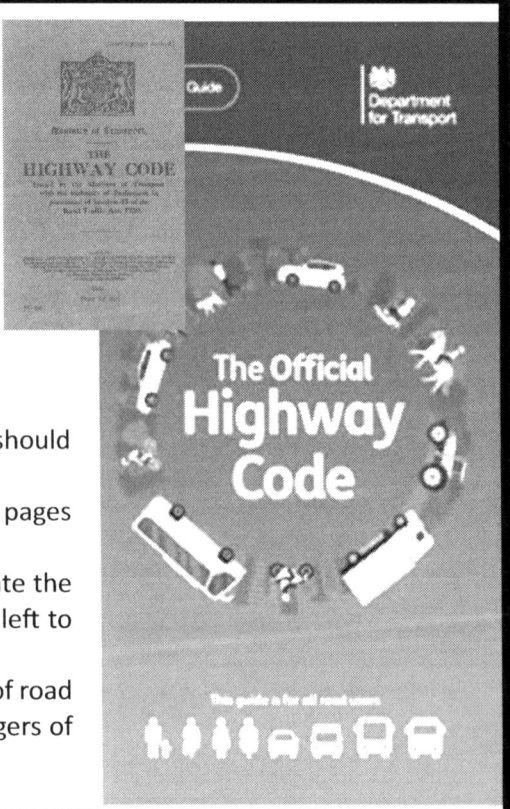

In July 1996 a separate written theory test was introduced to the Driving Test in the UK to replace questions asked about 'The Highway Code' whilst actually driving. Learner drivers were expected to know rather different information then from that published in the first edition of the Highway Code, price 1d, launched in 1931.

• In 1931 mirrors were not even mentioned.

• Drivers were advised to sound their horn when overtaking.

• At least 8 pages showed the various hand signals a driver should use. There was a single page in the current edition.

• Contained 18 pages (out of 24) of advice, compared to 135 pages in 2007.

• Included advice to drivers of horse drawn vehicles to 'rotate the whip above the head; then incline the whip to the right or left to show the direction in which the turn is to be made'.

It wasn't until the second edition of the Code that diagrams of road signs appeared, just 10 in all, plus a warning about the dangers of driving when tired or drinking and driving.

Renault Clio

Advertising for the first-generation Renault Clio introduced us to 'Nicole *et* Papa' and gave the small car a personality that appealed to drivers of all ages.

Ford Focus

The Focus replaced the previously very successful Escort. Ford wanted a 'World Car' to sell across all markets so the Focus was born and is still produced.

Toyota Previa

Toyota created the multi- purpose vehicle market with the Spacecruiser in the 80s, but the futuristic replacement, the Toyota Previa was a whole new approach to the people carrier.

Lexus LS 400

Toyota moved into the luxury market with the Lexus brand. The Lexus' flagship model is one of the most reliable vehicles ever built.

COCOTAXI

The auto-rickshaw began in Havana in the 1990s and soon spread to the whole of Cuba. These gas-scooters are named after their shape, that of a coconut and are made of a fibreglass shell with seats welded onto it. They can travel at about 30mph and because they are small, they weave and squeeze in and out of the city traffic. Blue Cocotaxis are for locals, yellow for tourists.

MOTORCYCLES

During the 1990s motorcycles started to evolve more quickly and there was a resurgence in the British biking industry with Triumph starting up production.

A bike lovers favourite however, was the 1995, Aprilia RS250.

New Year's Eve 1999
The Millennium Bug

Whilst the world was getting 'ready to party' there was an undercurrent of anxiety about the Y2K (year 2000) Bug and many people were scared. When complicated computer programmes were first written in the 1960s, programmers used a two-digit code for the year, leaving out the "19." As the year 2000 approached, many believed that the systems would not interpret the "00" correctly, making the year 2000 indistinguishable from 1900 causing a major malfunction.

It was particularly worrying to certain organisations. Banks calculate the rate for interest owed daily and instead of the rate for one day, if the 'clocks went back' their computers would calculate a rate of interest for **minus** 100 years!

Airlines felt they were at a very great risk. All scheduled flights are recorded on computers and liable to be affected and, if the computer reverted to 1900, well, there were very few airline flights that year!
Power plants were threatened, depending on routine computer maintenance for safety checks, such as water pressure or radiation levels, the wrong date would wreck the calculations and possibly put nearby residents at risk.

Huge sums were spent to prepare for the consequences and both software and hardware companies raced to fix it by developing "Y2K compliant" programmes. Midnight passed on the 1 January 2000 and the crisis failed to materialise - planes did not fall from the sky, power stations did not melt down and thousands of people who had stocked up on food, water, even arms, or purchased backup generators or withdrawn large sums of money in anticipation of a computer-induced apocalypse, could breathe easily again.

The Millennium Dome

Officially called the O2, the huge construction and tourist attraction alongside the Thames in Greenwich, London was initially built to house an exhibition for the approach of the 21st Century. Designed by Sir Richard Rogers, the central dome is the largest in the world. On December 31, 1999, a New Year's Eve celebration at the dome was attended by some 10,500 people, including the Prime Minister, Tony Blair, and the Queen. Opening the next day, the Millennium Dome exhibition lasted until December 31, 2000.

AND A NEW MILLENNIUM

Memorabilia and Monuments

The Millennium Wheel Better known as the London Eye, at 135m (443 ft) it is Europe's tallest cantilevered observation wheel. Situated on the South Bank of the Thames when opened it used to offer the highest public viewing point in London until superseded in 2013 by the 245m high (804 ft) observation deck on the 72nd floor of The Shard.

Portsmouth's Millennium Tower opened five years late and officials were so concerned that people may actually have forgotten what the millennium was, that they gave it a new name, **The Spinnaker Tower**.

The Millennium Bridge is a steel suspension bridge for pedestrians over the River Thames linking Bankside with the City of London. Londoners nicknamed it the "Wobbly Bridge" after pedestrians experienced an alarming swaying motion on its opening day.

Lots of memorabilia was produced to mark the new millennium.
Some pieces are timeless classics and others will soon be forgotten.

KEY EVENTS 2000-2009

2000:

Jan: Celebrations take place throughout the UK on the 1st and the Millennium Dome is officially opened by The Queen.

Aug 4th: Queen Elizabeth the Queen Mother celebrates her hundredth birthday

2001:

Feb: The Foot and Mouth disease crisis begins. Over 6 million cows and sheep are killed to halt the disease.

Jun: Labour wins the General Election. David Cameron is a new entrant, Edward Heath retires, and William Hague resigns as leader of the Conservatives.

2002:

Jan: The Euro is officially introduced in the Eurozone countries.

Jun: The Golden Jubilee. A special service is held in St Paul's Cathedral to mark the Queen's 50 years on the throne. Celebrations take place all over the country.

2003:

Mar: The United States, along with coalition forces primarily from the United Kingdom, initiates war on Iraq

May: BBC Radio 4 airs a report stating that the government claimed in its dossier, that Iraq could deploy weapons of mass destruction within forty-five minutes knowing the claim to be dubious.

Jul: Dr David Kelly, the weapons expert who was the reporter's source, is found dead.

2004:

Jan: The Hutton Inquiry into the circumstances of the death of Dr Kelly is published. The UK media, in general, condemns the report as a whitewash.

Jul: A new Countryside Code is published in advance of the 'Right to Roam' coming into effect in September across England and Wales.

TERRORISM

2001: On the 11th September, Al-Qaeda terrorists hijack civilian airliners and fly two into the Twin Towers of the World Trade Centre in New York, which collapse. There are 3,000 fatalities including 67 British nationals.

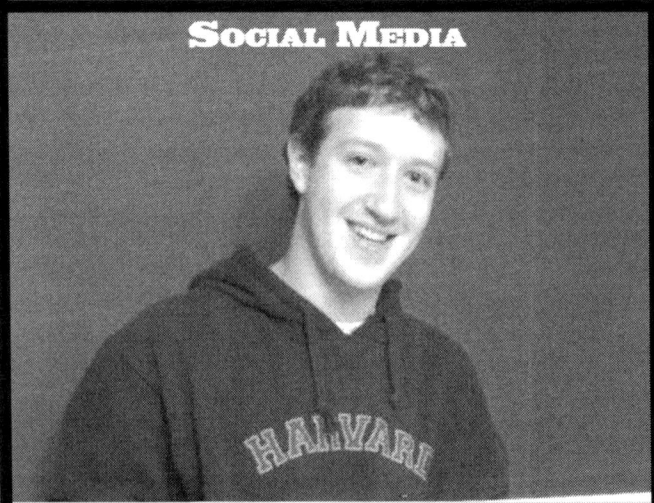

SOCIAL MEDIA

2004: In February, Mark Zuckerberg launches 'The Facebook', later renamed 'Facebook' as an online social networking website for Harvard University Students. In 2006 it was opened up to anyone over the age of 13.

EXPLOSION

2005: On the morning of 11 December, the UK experienced its largest explosion since World War Two. A huge blast at the Buncefield fuel depot in Hemel Hempstead, was heard as far away as the Netherlands and caused the UK's biggest blaze in peacetime which shrouded much of south-east England in smoke.

HIGH SPEED TRAINS

2007: In November, the Queen officially opened 'High Speed 1' and 'St Pancras International' station. The Channel Tunnel first opened to Eurostar in 1994, with trains running from Waterloo, but the new 69-mile link meant the journey from London to Paris reduced to 2 hrs 15 minutes and to Brussels 1 hr 51 min.

2005:

Apr: Prince Charles marries Camilla Parker Bowles at a private ceremony at Windsor Guildhall.

Aug: Hurricane Katrina devastates much of the U.S. Gulf Coast from Louisiana to the Florida Panhandle killing an estimated 1,836 people

2006:

Jul: Twitter is launched, becoming one of the largest social media platforms in the world.

Nov: Alexander Litvinenko a British-naturalised Russian defector dies of polonium poisoning in London.

2007:

Jun: Tony Blair resigns as Prime Minister and Gordon Brown is elected unopposed.

Jul: England introduces a ban on smoking in enclosed public places in line with Scotland, Wales and N. Ireland.

2008:

Mar: Terminal 5 is opened at London Heathrow but IT problems cause over 500 flights to be cancelled

Nov: St Hilda's College admits male undergraduates and ceases to be the last single-sex college at Oxford.

Dec: Woolworths shuts down in the UK.

2009:

Jul: The largest haul of Anglo-Saxon treasure ever found, the Staffordshire Hoard, is first uncovered buried beneath a field near Litchfield. 4,600 items amounting to 11 lb of gold, 3lb of silver and 3.5k pieces of garnet cloisonné jewellery.

Oct: The independent audit of MPs expenses is completed and exposes a widespread parliamentary scandal.

2010:

Jan: In the Chilcott Inquiry, set up in 2009, Tony Blair is questioned in public for the first time about his decision to take the UK to war against Iraq.

May: The General Election results in a Hung Parliament. An alliance is formed between the Tories and the Liberal Democrats.

2011:

Feb: An earthquake of 6.3 magnitude devastates Christchurch, New Zealand. Hundreds of people are killed.

Apr: Prince William marries Catherine Middleton in Westminster Abbey.

2012:

Jun: The UK begins celebrations of the Queen's Diamond Jubilee. Events include a pageant on the Thames and a Pop Concert outside Buckingham Palace

Jul: The summer Olympic Games are held in London, making it the first city to host them for a third time.

2013:

Jul: A new Marriage Act receives Royal Assent and same-sex marriage becomes legal in England and Wales.

Aug: A burger, grown from bovine stem cells in a laboratory, is cooked and eaten in London. The same month, a 15 ton 'fatburg' is removed after completely blocking a London sewer.

2014:

Mar: Prince Harry launches the Invictus Games for wounded soldiers.

Mar: The first gay weddings take place in England and Wales.

THE SHARD

2012: In July, The Shard, an iconic 'vertical city' is officially opened in London. It is the tallest building in Europe and the tallest habitable free-standing structure in the UK at 1,016ft (309.6 m)

THE ARAB SPRING

2010: 'The Arab Spring', a series of anti-government protests, uprisings, and armed rebellions spread across much of the Arab world. Starting in Tunisia it spread to Libya, Egypt, Yemen, Syria and Bahrain. Amongst leaders to be deposed was Gaddafi of Libya.

BREXIT

June 2016: After months of heated, angry argument and debate, the referendum on whether to leave the EU or remain within it, is held. Nearly 30m people take part and the result is to leave the EU: 51.9% votes to 48.1%.

March 2017: Article 50 is invoked and the two-year countdown to departure begins.

March 2019: Parliament rejected Theresa May's EU withdrawal agreement and a new deadline is set by The European Council to leave, with or without an Agreement, at the end of Oct 2019.

Jun 2019: Unable to 'deliver Brexit', Theresa May steps down and in Jul 2019: Boris Johnson becomes Prime Minister.

Oct 2019: The deadline to leave passes, and the EU agrees to a new date, end of Jan 2020. Commemorative Brexit coins are melted down.

Jan 2020: Johnson signs the Withdrawal Agreement.

January 31ˢᵗ 2020: At 11pm, the UK leaves the European Union and marks the moment with a party in Parliament Square.

2015:
Jan: Two Al-Qaeda gunmen kill 12 and injure 11 more at the Paris headquarters of the satirical newspaper Charlie Hebdo.

May: The General Election is won by David Cameron for the Conservatives with an outright majority of 331 seats.
Jun: The 800th anniversary of the Magna Carta.

2016:
Jun: The UK Referendum to leave the EU, Brexit, takes place and the majority vote is 'Yes'. David Cameron later resigns.
Jul: On July 14, Bastille Day (Independence Day), a terrorist drives a truck through a crowded promenade in Nice, France. 87 people are killed.
Nov: Donald Trump becomes US President.

2017:
There are a string of deadly terror attacks in Britain including : Westminster Bridge, the Manchester Arena and London Bridge.
Jun: The Tories lose their majority in Theresa May's general election gamble.

2018:
Apr: The UK, France, and United States order the bombing of Syrian military bases.

May: Prince Harry marries the American actress Meghan Markle in St George's Chapel, Windsor Castle. It is thought 1.9m people watched on TV worldwide.

2019:
Jun: Theresa May resigns as Prime Minister. Before she goes, she agrees a new legally binding target to reach net zero by 2050.
Jul: Boris Johnson becomes Prime Minister.

1945 Calendar

January

S	M	T	W	T	F	S
	1	2	3	4	5	6
7	8	9	10	11	12	13
14	15	16	17	18	19	20
21	22	23	24	25	26	27
28	29	30	31			

February

S	M	T	W	T	F	S
				1	2	3
4	5	6	7	8	9	10
11	12	13	14	15	16	17
18	19	20	21	22	23	24
25	26	27	28			

March

S	M	T	W	T	F	S
				1	2	3
4	5	6	7	8	9	10
11	12	13	14	15	16	17
18	19	20	21	22	23	24
25	26	27	28	29	30	31

April

S	M	T	W	T	F	S
1	2	3	4	5	6	7
8	9	10	11	12	13	14
15	16	17	18	19	20	21
22	23	24	25	26	27	28
29	30					

May

S	M	T	W	T	F	S
		1	2	3	4	5
6	7	8	9	10	11	12
13	14	15	16	17	18	19
20	21	22	23	24	25	26
27	28	29	30	31		

June

S	M	T	W	T	F	S
					1	2
3	4	5	6	7	8	9
10	11	12	13	14	15	16
17	18	19	20	21	22	23
24	25	26	27	28	29	30

July

S	M	T	W	T	F	S
1	2	3	4	5	6	7
8	9	10	11	12	13	14
15	16	17	18	19	20	21
22	23	24	25	26	27	28
29	30	31				

August

S	M	T	W	T	F	S
		1	2	3	4	
5	6	7	8	9	10	11
12	13	14	15	16	17	18
19	20	21	22	23	24	25
26	27	28	29	30	31	

September

S	M	T	W	T	F	S
						1
2	3	4	5	6	7	8
9	10	11	12	13	14	15
16	17	18	19	20	21	22
23	24	25	26	27	28	29
30						

October

S	M	T	W	T	F	S
	1	2	3	4	5	6
7	8	9	10	11	12	13
14	15	16	17	18	19	20
21	22	23	24	25	26	27
28	29	30	31			

November

S	M	T	W	T	F	S
				1	2	3
4	5	6	7	8	9	10
11	12	13	14	15	16	17
18	19	20	21	22	23	24
25	26	27	28	29	30	

December

S	M	T	W	T	F	S
						1
2	3	4	5	6	7	8
9	10	11	12	13	14	15
16	17	18	19	20	21	22
23	24	25	26	27	28	29
30	31					

Printed in Great Britain
by Amazon

2f0b6bdd-c83b-4e4a-ac15-b63bf069bfd0R01